Praise for Richard Russo's

Elsewhere

"Redemption is always the prize in a Russo story. Nowhere do we see that more clearly than in *Elsewhere*, a brave little book in which a writer spins deprivation into advantage, suffering into wisdom, and a broken mother into a muse."
—*The Washington Post*

"Vivid. . . . Devastating. . . . Russo brings the remarkable compassion he's known for in his fiction to this account."
—*The Christian Science Monitor*

"Russo is the Bruce Springsteen of novelists. . . . In a paragraph or even a phrase, he can summon up a whole world."
—Maureen Corrigan, *Fresh Air*

"Funny and winning. . . . This stirring book belongs to Jean and Rick."   —*The New York Times Book Review*

"Filled with insights, by turn tender and tough, about human fidelity, frailty, forbearance, and fortitude."
—*The Philadelphia Inquirer*

"A quietly riveting portrait. . . . *Elsewhere* depicts the tenacious grip that Gloversville exerted on mother and son alike."
—*The New York Observer*

"Exquisite. . . . *Elsewhere* is a memoir and a bravura essay, a meditation on negotiating flaws."   —*The Miami Herald*

"Richard Russo has mined his childhood with enormous energy, humor and craftsmanship. . . . Readers discovering Russo through this memoir and then returning to his first few titles are embarking on a delightful voyage with a gifted writer about whom they now know a great deal."
—*The Seattle Times*

"Affecting. . . . Russo's parallel themes of people and place come together elegantly."   —*San Francisco Chronicle*

"A real-life mystery about his mother's demons. . . . Russo writes without bitterness, but with the kind of clear-eyed compassion he bestows on his fictional characters."
—*USA Today*

"Rich and layered . . . Russo's memoir is an honest book about a universal subject: those familial bonds that only get trickier with time."   —*Minneapolis Star Tribune*

"Outstanding."   —*Chicago Sun-Times*

RICHARD RUSSO

Elsewhere

Richard Russo lives with his wife in Camden,
Maine, and Boston. In 2002 he was awarded
the Pulitzer Prize for *Empire Falls*.

ALSO BY RICHARD RUSSO

Mohawk

The Risk Pool

Nobody's Fool

Straight Man

Empire Falls

The Whore's Child

Bridge of Sighs

That Old Cape Magic

Interventions

Elsewhere

Elsewhere

RICHARD RUSSO

Vintage Books
A Division of Random House, Inc.
New York

FIRST VINTAGE BOOKS EDITION, JULY 2013

The Library of Congress has cataloged the Knopf edition as follows:
Russo, Richard.
Elsewhere / by Richard Russo. — 1st ed.
p. cm.
1. Russo, Richard, 1949—Family. 2. Russo, Richard, 1949—
Childhood and youth. 3. Novelists, American—Biography.
4. Gloversville (N.Y.)—Biography. I. Title.
PS3568.U812Z46 2012
813'.54—dc23
[B] 2012016354

Vintage ISBN: 978-0-307-94976-9

Book design by Cassandra J. Pappas

www.vintagebooks.com

Printed in the United States of America
10 9 8 7 6 5 4 3 2 1

For Greg

Elsewhere

Prologue

A few years ago, passing the sign on the New York State Thru-way for the Central Leatherstocking Region, a friend of mine misread it as saying *laughingstock* and thought, That must be where Russo's from. She was right. I'm from Gloversville, just a few miles north in the foothills of the Adirondacks, a place that's easy to joke about unless you live there, as some of my family still do.

The town wasn't always a joke. In its heyday, nine out of ten dress gloves in the United States were manufactured there. By the end of the nineteenth century, craftsmen from all over Europe had flocked in, for decades producing gloves on a par with the finest made anywhere in the world. Back then glove-cutting was governed by a guild, and you typically apprenticed, as my maternal grandfather did, for two or three years. The primary tools of a trained glove-cutter's trade were his eye, his experience of animal skins, and his imagination. It was my grandfather who gave me my first lessons in art—though I doubt he would've worded it like that—when he explained the challenge of making something truly fine and beautiful from an imperfect hide. After they're tanned but before they go to the cutter, skins are rolled and brushed and finished to ensure smooth uniformity, but inevitably they retain some of nature's imperfections. The true craftsman, he gave me to understand, works around these flaws or figures out how to incorporate them into the glove's natural folds or stitching. Each skin posed problems whose resolution required creativity. The glove-cutter's job wasn't just to get as many gloves as possible out of a hide but to do so while minimizing its flaws.

Leather had been tanned in Fulton County, using the bark of hemlock trees, since before the American Revolution. Gloversville and neighboring Johnstown were home not only to gloves but to all things leather: shoes and coats and handbags and upholstery. My paternal grandfather, from Salerno, Italy, having heard about this place where so many artisans had gathered, journeyed to upstate New York in hopes of making a living there as a shoemaker. From New York City he took the train north to Albany, then west as far as the Barge Canal hamlet of Fonda, where he followed the freight tracks north up to Johnstown, where I was born decades later. Did he have any real idea of where he was headed, or what his new life would be like? You tell me. Among the few material possessions he brought with him from the old country was an opera cape.

Both men had wretched timing. My father's father soon learned that Fulton County wasn't Manhattan or even Salerno, and that few men in his new home would buy expensive custom-made shoes instead of cheaper machine-made ones, so he had little choice but to become a shoe repairman. And by the time my mother's father arrived in Gloversville from Vermont, the real craft of glove-cutting was already under assault. By the end of World War I, many gloves were being "pattern cut." (For a size 6 glove, a size 6 pattern was affixed to the skin and cut around with shears.) Once he returned from World War II, the process was largely mechanized by "clicker-cutting" machines that quickly stamped out presized gloves, requiring the operator only to position the tanned skin under the machine's lethal blades and pull down on its mechanical arm. I was born in 1949, by which time there wasn't much demand for handmade gloves or shoes, but both my grandfathers had long since made their big moves to Fulton County and staked their dubious claims. By then they had families, and so there they remained. It was also during the first half of the twentieth century that chrome tanning, a chemical procedure that made leather more supple and water resistant, and dramatically sped up the whole process, became the industry standard, replacing traditional vegetable tanning and making tanneries even more hazardous, not just for workers but also for those who lived nearby and, especially, downstream. Speed, efficiency, and technology had trumped art and craft, not to mention public safety.

That said, between 1890 and 1950 people in Gloversville made good money, some of them a lot of it. Drive along Kingsboro Avenue, which parallels Main Street, and have a gander at the fine old houses set back from the street and well apart from one another, and you'll get a sense of the prosperity that at least the fortunate ones enjoyed until World War II. Even downtown Gloversville, which by the 1970s had become a Dresden-like ruin, still shows signs of that wealth. The Andrew Carnegie Gloversville Free Library is as lovely as can be, and the old high school, which sits atop a gentle hill, bespeaks a community that believed both in itself and that good times would not be fleeting. On its sloping lawn stands a statue of Lucius Nathan Littauer, one of the richest men in the county, whose extended arm appears to point at the grand marble edifice of the nearby Eccentric Club, which refused him membership because he was a Jew. Down the street is the recently restored Glove Theatre, where I spent just about every Saturday afternoon of my adolescence. There was also a charming old hotel, the Kingsboro, in whose elegant dining room Monsignor Kreugler, whom I'd served as an altar boy at Sacred Heart Church, held weekly court after his last Sunday Mass. Once it was razed, visitors had to stay in nearby Johnstown, out on the arterial highway that was supposed to breathe new life into Gloversville but instead, all too predictably, allowed people to race by, without stopping or even slowing down, en route to Saratoga, Lake George, or Montreal.

How quickly it all happened. In the Fifties, on a Saturday afternoon, the streets downtown would be gridlocked with cars honking hellos at pedestrians. The sidewalks were so jammed with shoppers that, as a boy trapped among taller adults, I had to depend on my mother, herself no giant, to navigate us from one store to the next or, more harrowingly, across Main Street. Often, when we finished what we called our weekly "errands," my mother and I would stop in at Pedrick's. Located next to city hall, it was a dark, cool place, the only establishment of my youth that was air-conditioned, with a long, thin wall whose service window allowed sodas and cocktails to be passed from the often raucous bar into the more respectable restaurant. Back then Pedrick's was always mobbed, even in the middle of a Saturday afternoon. Mounted on the wall of each booth was a minijukebox whose movable mechanical pages were full of song listings. Selections made here—five for a quarter, if memory serves—were played on the real jukebox on the far wall. We always played a whole quarter's worth while nursing sodas served so cold they made my teeth hurt. Sometimes, though, the music was drowned out by rowdy male laughter from the bar, where the wall-mounted television was tuned to a Yankees ball game, and if anybody hit a home run everyone in the restaurant knew it immediately. I remember listening intently to all the men's voices, trying to pick out my father's. He and my mother had separated when I was little, but he was still around town, and I always imagined him on the other side of that wall in Pedrick's.

I also suspected that my mother, if she hadn't been saddled with me, would have preferred to be over there herself. She liked men, liked being among them, and on the restaurant side it was mostly women and kids and older people. Though I couldn't have put it into words, I had the distinct impression that the wall separating respectability from fun was very thin indeed. There was another jukebox in the bar, and sometimes it got cranked up loud enough to compete with whatever was playing on ours, and then my mother would say it was time to go, as if she feared the wall itself might come crashing down. To her, music getting pumped up like that could only mean one thing: that people were dancing, middle of the afternoon or not, and if she'd been over there, she would've been as well. A good decade after the end of World War II, Gloversville was still in a party mode, and regular Saturday festivities routinely continued right up to last call and often beyond, the town's prosperous citizens dancing and drinking at the Eccentric Club, the more middle-class folk in the blue-collar taverns along upper Main Street or, in summer, at the pavilion at nearby Caroga Lake, the poor (often the most recent immigrants with the lowest-paying tannery jobs) in the gin mills bordering South Main in the section of town referred to as "the Gut," where arrests for drunkenness or indecency or belligerence were much more likely to be recorded in the local newspaper on Monday than comparable exploits at the Eccentric Club.

By the time I graduated from high school in 1967, you could have strafed Main Street with an automatic weapon without endangering a soul. On Saturday afternoons the sidewalks were deserted, people in newly reduced circumstances shopping for bargains at the cheap, off-brand stores that had sprung up along the arterial. The marquee at the Glove Theatre bore the title of the last film to play there, though enough of the letters were missing that you couldn't guess what it was. Jobless men emerged from the pool hall or one of the seedy gin mills that sold cheap draft beer and rotgut rye, blinking into the afternoon light and flexing at the knees. Lighting up a smoke, they'd peer up Main Street in one direction, then down the other, as if wondering where the hell everybody went. By then the restaurant side of Pedrick's had closed, but since I turned eighteen that summer, now of legal drinking age, the other side was no longer off-limits. Now, though, it was quiet as a library. The Yankees were still playing on the television, but Mantle and Maris and Yogi and Whitey Ford had all retired, and their glory days, like Gloversville's, were over. The half-dozen grizzled, solitary drinkers rotated on their stools when the door opened, like the past might saunter in out of the bright glare trailing ten-dollar bills in its wake. Every now and then that summer of '67, I'd poke my head into Pedrick's to see if my father was among those drinking Utica Club drafts at the bar. But, like time itself, he, too, had moved on.

WHAT HAPPENED? Lots of things. After World War II, about when men stopped wearing hats, women stopped wearing gloves. Jackie Kennedy did wear a pair at her husband's inauguration, and that turned the clock back for a while, but the trend proved irreversible. More important, glove making started going overseas where labor was cheap. Gloversville went bust the way Mike Campbell declares his bankruptcy in Hemingway's *The Sun Also Rises,* "gradually and then suddenly." The "giant sucking sound" of globalism arrived decades early and with a vengeance. My maternal grandfather, who, despite being a veteran of two world wars, had been branded a Communist from the pulpit of Sacred Heart Church for being a union man, saw it coming even before crappy Asian-made gloves showed up in the shops, where a few buttons could be sewn on and the gloves stamped MADE IN GLOVERSVILLE. Around Thanksgiving, the trade's off-season, workers in the skin mills got laid off, and every year it took a little longer for them to be called back. Worse, they weren't all rehired at once, which practice allowed the shop owners to remind their employees that things were different now. What mattered was moving inventory down the line, not quality. After all, Asians and Indians were doing what the local stiffs did for a quarter of the cost.

My grandfather, who came home from the Pacific with malaria and soon afterward developed emphysema, was by then too sick to fight. He continued to work as always, refusing to cut corners and, as a result, making considerably less money than men for whom slapdash was good enough. The bosses could exploit him, give him the most flawed skins, and treat him like a robot instead of the craftsman he was, but he claimed the one thing they couldn't order him to do was a bad job. But of course they didn't need to. You only had to look at how his narrow, concave chest heaved as he struggled to draw oxygen into his failing lungs to know he wouldn't be anybody's problem much longer. His wife, who'd also survived the Depression, foresaw a diminished future. She began stocking the pantry with cans of wax beans and tuna fish earlier every year, aware that the layoffs would run even longer, and her husband, growing sicker by the day, would be among the last called back. Jesus on his best day could do no more with loaves and fishes than my grandmother did with a pound of bacon. Still, it was just a matter of time.

None of which had much effect on me. As a boy I was happy as a clam in Gloversville. My mother and I shared a modest two-family house on Helwig Street with her parents. They lived in the two-bedroom, single-bath downstairs flat, my mother and I in the identically configured one above. My grandfather, who'd never before purchased anything he couldn't pay for with cash out of his wallet, bought the house, I suspect, because he knew his daughter's marriage was on the rocks and that she and I would need a place to live. Our block of Helwig Street was neighborly, with a corner grocery store situated diagonally across the street. My mother's sister and her family lived around the corner on Sixth Avenue, which meant I grew up surrounded by cousins. In kindergarten and first grade, my grandmother walked me to school in the morning and was there to meet me in the afternoon, and in the summer we took walks to a lovely little park a few blocks away. On weekends it was often my grandfather who'd take my hand, and together we'd head downtown for a bag of "peatles," his peculiar word for red-skinned peanuts, stopping on the way back to visit with friends sitting out on their porches. By the time I was old enough to get my first bike and explore beyond Helwig Street, I'd discovered the magic of baseball, and so, wooden bat over my shoulder, mitt dangling from my handlebars, I disappeared with friends for whole mornings or afternoons or both. At my aunt's there was a hoop over the garage, and during the long winters my cousin Greg and I kept the driveway shoveled meticulously so we could shoot baskets, even when it was so cold the net froze and you couldn't dribble the ball. Come autumn I raked leaves, stealing this job from my grandfather, who loved to do it, though he didn't always have sufficient breath. Sometimes he'd start the job, and I'd finish while he snuck a cigarette around back of the house where my grandmother couldn't see him. Summers I mowed lawns, and winters I shoveled sidewalks. An American childhood, as lived in the Fifties by a lower-middle class that seems barely to exist anymore, in a town that seemed unexceptional then, and not, as it seems to me now, the canary in the mine shaft.

WHAT FOLLOWS in this memoir—I don't know what else to call it—is a story of intersections: of place and time, of private and public, of linked destinies and flawed devotion. It's more my mother's story than mine, but it's mine, too, because until just a few years ago she was seldom absent from my life. It's about her character but also about where she grew up, fled from, and returned to again and again, about contradictions she couldn't resolve and so passed on to me, knowing full well I'd worry them much like a dog worries a bone, gnawing, burying, unearthing, gnawing again, until there's nothing left but sharp splinters and bleeding gums.

I keep returning to that wall in Pedrick's, the one separating the restaurant from the bar. How close she was to where she wanted to be. How flimsy that wall must've seemed, the music and laughter leaking through so easily. But then my mother was forever misjudging—not just distance and direction but the sturdiness of the barriers erected between her and what she so desperately desired. I should know. I was one of them.

Independence

THE NIGHT BEFORE we scattered my mother's ashes in Menemsha Pond on Martha's Vineyard, I had a dream in which she featured vividly. She'd been visiting my sleep regularly since her death in July, and it was now the last week of December. Was there some duty other than the scattering of her ashes that I'd left undone? Some other subconscious reason for her to pay me a visit? A lot had happened since July. I'd gone on a long book tour, our daughter Kate had been married in London over Thanksgiving, and we'd returned home just in time for the hustle and bustle of Christmas. Was she feeling abandoned? That, of course, was another way of asking whether I was feeling guilty about neglecting her in death as I sometimes worried I'd done in life.

We'd delayed scattering her ashes for so long because both my daughters wanted to be present. Emily had recently started a new job at a bookstore near Amherst and didn't feel she could request time off until after the holiday rush. And Kate and her husband, Tom, still very much newlyweds, couldn't get a flight to the States until after Christmas. Thus we convened on the island during the week between Christmas and New Year's to make good on what I'd come to think of as my final promise to my mother, the last in a long, unbroken string of obligations that extended back almost as far as I could remember.

In the dream my mother and I were on foot, heading toward some vague destination we'd apparently agreed on. That we were going at all must have been my idea, because I was feeling particularly guilty about how long it was taking, and for not knowing the way and taking several wrong turns. Of course, getting my mother, who didn't drive, to wherever she needed to be—the grocery store, the doctor's office, the hairdresser's—had been my responsibility, off and on, since I got my driver's license in 1967, so in that sense my dream was cribbing from reality. That I was lost was a more unusual and troubling aspect of the narrative, since I'd always been the one responsible for knowing the way. My mother's poor sense of direction was legendary, and it long had been a joke between us that she was a compass whose needle pointed due south. No doubt my feeling lost and helpless in the dream had to do with her real-life condition during the long months before her death. Diagnosed with congestive heart disease, she'd been given two years at the outside, which meant that for the first time in decades she was going somewhere on her own.

In the dream she wasn't dying, just weak and fatigued as we

soldiered on through the darkening streets, looking for signs or landmarks where there weren't any. Finally, she was unable to go on, and I had to carry her. Initially, this wasn't a problem. My mother had always been petite, and now she was frail, while I was strong from tennis and running. But gradually I began to feel her exhaustion, as well as her frustration with me for landing us in this predicament. There were just the two of us in empty streets that stretched on forever, with no option but to slog ahead.

That was the dream. My mother and I going on and on, forever and ever, until finally I awoke to the old knowledge that she'd been dead since the summer, that in reality the burden of her long illness and longer unhappiness had at last been lifted from her shoulders. And from my own.

Some dreams require no interpretation, and this was one of them.

FROM THE TIME I was a boy, my mother valued few things more than her perceived independence. The legal separation she'd negotiated with my father stipulated that he contribute to my maintenance, though he seldom did. For a while she tried to compel him but quickly gave up, probably figuring that in the long run she was better off. Even if he wasn't helping out, at least she wasn't saddled with his gambling debts. She paid rent to my grandparents—at market price, she always proudly claimed—for our flat in their house on Helwig Street. Her job at GE in Schenectady paid well; before taxes she made just over a hundred dollars a week, more than many of the men who worked in the skin mills. Most women in Gloversville who worked were sewing gloves in the shops or at home, underpaid piecework that complemented the earnings of husbands who got laid off every winter and whose wages otherwise were kept artificially low through the collusion of the mill owners and the local government they held sway over. She was much better off working for a big company in Schenectady, though there were attendant expenses. For one thing she was a professional woman and had to dress like one. That suited her fine, because she loved nice clothes, but of course they weren't cheap. Also, because she got home from work too late and too exhausted to cook, she had to pay my grandparents for my board. Then there was the cost of her ride to and from GE with coworkers; when we went places with my aunt and uncle and cousins, she always made a point of chipping in for gas.

She ferociously defended her hard-earned independence against all comers, even (and especially) my grandparents, who were in many respects its true source. In particular she didn't appreciate unsolicited advice about my upbringing, and when they crossed that line she reminded them that theirs was primarily a financial arrangement. She paid her rent, promptly, the first of each month, which to her way of thinking meant they had no more right to intrude into our lives than any other landlord. If her parents were ever angered or hurt by the curtness of this, they never said so, at least not in front of me, but who could have blamed them? After all, my grandfather had bought the house, at least in part, so my mother and I would have someplace to live. To my knowledge they never reminded her of this, and she clearly saw it differently. She let it be known there were lots of places for rent in both Gloversville and Schenectady, and if her parents couldn't mind their own business, she'd move into one and take me with her. I don't doubt my mother's threat was sincere—when angry she was always sincere—but there wasn't much danger of her following through, and my grandparents must have known that, too. "*Jean,*" one of them would say when she got on her high horse, and I'd think that this time they were going to have it out with her for sure, but then they'd look at me and let their voices fall.

Gradually I came to understand that my mother's seeming ingratitude was simply self-preservation. Her view of herself as a woman who could get things done on her own required constant tending and bolstering. She had to assert her independence, to say the words out loud, at every opportunity, if she herself was to believe it. She had to remind herself constantly that she had a *good* job at a *great* company in a *real* city. Not just a job, but a better, more responsible *position* than just about any other woman in Gloversville. She not only paid her own way in the world but also fed, clothed, and raised me. Moreover, she was broadening my horizons beyond the smug, complacent, self-satisfied, dimwitted ethos of the ugly little mill town we lived in. Tired as she was at the end of her long day, she made sure I'd finished my homework and done it well. If I brought home a form, she filled it out, never needing to be reminded, and if a check was to be attached for the rental of a uniform or a musical instrument, somehow she managed. I had clean, crisply ironed clothing to wear every day, even if it meant she had to stay up until midnight doing laundry. She would skip dinners to meet with my teachers to make sure I wasn't just learning in school but flourishing, that I wasn't being dismissed as an irrelevant, fatherless boy. These were real accomplishments. No other woman my mother knew struggled under such burdens or challenges, and she was doing it, she told herself, all by herself.

Except she wasn't, not really, and sometimes that terrible truth would punch through the defenses she'd erected and fortified at such a high personal cost. To her credit, she almost never shared her doubts, her temporary losses of faith, with me, her principal audience. She kept the narrative of our lives consistent and intact. We, the two of us, were all we needed. As long as we had each other, we'd be fine. For my part I never let on that I suspected the truth: that, yes, she had a good job, but that as a woman she was still paid less than men with the same duties. They had families to support, she was told, as if she didn't. By the time she paid for her ride to and from work and the clothes she needed to look the part there, she could have done almost as well working in Gloversville. Yes, she paid her rent faithfully, but at Gloversville, not Schenectady, prices, and my grandparents, though they never said so, could have charged anybody else more. And what would it have cost if she'd had to pay someone to look after me while she worked, a job my grandmother did, lovingly, for free?

Even so, most of the time she was able to make ends meet,

and our lives proceeded smoothly enough to maintain the necessary façade of independence. Every month my mother budgeted our expenses to the last penny, which meant that our cash flow was a frayed shoestring that occasionally snapped. Any surprise could push us into the red, and then she'd have to borrow from her parents, the very people she was forever claiming our independence from. Sometimes I grew too fast and needed new clothes sooner than she'd projected, or I'd tear a hole in a brand-new pair of pants climbing over the neighbors' fences on the way to school. Other times I'd *want* things. Big things. One Christmas my cousins got a *Book of Knowledge* encyclopedia, and she had to explain why we couldn't have one, how expensive it was, how long she'd have to work to pay for it, how many other things we needed more. And besides, I could use my cousins' whenever I needed to. Though I was just a boy, I knew that she was holding things together, holding herself together, by sheer force of will, that the cold facts bore down on her relentlessly. She always paid back the small loans my grandparents floated us, but their necessity undermined the cherished myth of independence. Our well-being, at least on occasion, was being subsidized. Not that any of this was her fault. My mother seldom mentioned my father, but in crisis she'd sometimes lament that the money we were short was exactly the sum he refused to pay.

Indeed, my father was a tricky subject. They'd separated not long after we moved to Helwig Street, and what little I knew about him was so contradictory I couldn't make sense of it. On the one hand he was a war hero. I knew what D-day was and that my father was there, at Utah Beach, and had fought his way through France and Germany all the way to Berlin. I knew he'd won a Bronze Star. My mother never minimized any of this. She said I should be proud of what he'd done in the war. But now he was a gambler, a man who couldn't be trusted to bring home his paycheck. He was the reason we sometimes got angry phone calls in the middle of the night. I wasn't to think badly of my father, though. His gambling was a sickness, and he couldn't help himself. He was trying to stop, but so far he couldn't.

What I knew about him paled by comparison to what I didn't. For instance, where did he live? I knew he was still in Gloversville because my mother said so, and my grandparents and my aunt Phyllis confirmed it. I associated him with the pool hall so strongly that for a while I imagined him living above it. When I asked my mother where he lived and who with, she said there was no telling. He wasn't like us. We lived in the same place and with the same people all the time. My father could be anywhere, with anybody. I assumed this must be tied somehow to his gambling. If there were always people looking for him, wanting their money back, then not having a regular address or a consistent group of friends meant he'd be harder to find. Still, it was difficult to square all this with his being a war hero. I wondered if one or the other might be a lie.

Of all the known facts about him, the one that was most significant to my mother was this: if he'd paid his due, his fair share, we'd be sitting pretty. That bitter logic seemed a comfort to her, as did the fact that she seldom needed help from him or anyone, and never needed much. She was making things work, almost.

HALF A CENTURY LATER, prior to her final illness, she was in much the same boat. In her eighties by then, she was living in Camden, Maine, a few short blocks from our house. When people asked if this Megunticook House was an assisted-living facility, she always replied, "Oh, *no*. I live independently."

Though she hasn't a mean-spirited bone in her body, this characterization always made my wife swallow hard. "What do you suppose she *means* when she says that?" Doing my best Wallace Shawn, I'd reply, "Inconceivable." *The Princess Bride* was one of our daughters' favorite movies growing up, and in it André the Giant says, referring to Shawn's character, "He uses that word a lot. I don't think it means what he thinks it does." Which was precisely my wife's point about my mother's claim of independence. After all, for the last thirty-five years we'd joked that we never went anywhere for longer than it took for her milk to spoil. Part of what my mother meant, of course, was that she wasn't living *with* us, in our house, but she also was proud that, for a woman her age, she was still spry and active. She took care of herself: made her grocery list and filled her basket only with what was on it; kept her own checkbook, paid her bills, and ordered clothes from catalogs over the phone, there being no place for an elderly woman who didn't want to look frumpy to shop along our stretch of the Maine coast. In fact, she had briefly tried assisted living but hated every minute of it—the phony cheer of group activities, the dining room's mushy, overcooked food and overheated conversation, the periodic, obligatory inspections of her apartment (*her* apartment!) to make sure she wasn't creating, as even she had to admit some of the other ladies did, some kind of fire hazard. My mother wanted none of that, and she was especially disdainful of the facility's other services: transportation to the grocery store ("My son does that"), to the doctor (ditto), the dentist (ditto again), and the hairdresser (and again). She didn't require a scooter and didn't need to hang on to anyone's arm or on to the ugly ubiquitous railings bolted to the corridor walls. She certainly didn't need to be wheeled anywhere. Despite chronic lower-back problems, she still cleaned her own bathtub and did her own ironing. Nor did she want me paying for it. We never showed her the bills, but she somehow found out that it cost about the same as a year's college tuition, and that was that.

So when she said she lived independently, she also meant—and this was another point of pride—that she received little financial help from us. And she had good reason to be proud. Having never in her life been well paid, her monthly Social Security check was meager in the extreme; and having divorced my father, she could lay no claim to his veteran's pension. She had no inheritance beyond her mother's Depression-era ability to stretch a budget, which owed much to a stubborn willingness to do without a lot of what other people considered necessities. She qualified for rent and heat assistance from the state, as well as food stamps, though she was too vain to accept these. Okay, there was a shortfall most months, just as there'd often been on Helwig Street, a shortfall that I, like any decent son who had the wherewithal, was happy to make up. And of course there was the occasional emergency. That said, the only times she and I ever argued about money was when I tried to give her more than she asked for, hoping to make her life a little easier. But she didn't *need* any more than I was giving her, she insisted. She took great pride, she explained, just as she had always done, in taking care of herself.

In the end, of course, after her health began to seriously fail and her needs grew exponentially, month to month, she'd take my hand and say, "What would I do without you?" I tried to reassure her by saying, "That's what I'm here for," and reminding her that, unlike far too many writers, I made an excellent living. To which she'd reply that, yes, of course she knew. She guessed it was still pretty much like the old days on Helwig Street. As long as we had each other, things would be fine. But then, anxious, she'd look around her apartment, at her increasingly constricting world, and say, "But if anything ever happened to you, I'd have to say good-bye to my independence."

AS A YOUNGER WOMAN my mother didn't see her inability to drive as inconsistent with her desire to be, and to be seen as, a bold and independent woman. Gloversville was a walkable town with small markets on every other corner, and in the postwar years lots of people still viewed cars as extravagances, though that was rapidly changing. My grandparents didn't own one, and neither did other people in the neighborhood. But there was also the gender issue. My aunt and uncle had a car, but she didn't drive, and of course my grandmother didn't either, though as married women independence wasn't a hook they were hanging their hats on. Driving was something men did. The fact that after separating from my father my mother didn't *have* a man anymore was to her irrelevant. All over America, men returning from the war were moving with their families into the suburbs, where their wives discovered they had to learn to drive or be trapped in their dream houses, but in Gloversville there was no such necessity. More to the point, my mother possessed another skill that was even more valuable than the ability to drive a car, and that was her ability to convince other people to take us where we needed to go.

That's how it had been when we visited Martha's Vineyard when I was ten, perhaps the most astonishing and luxurious occasion of my childhood. My mother thought the resort she'd chosen provided everything we'd need—food, drink, plenty of activities for a boy my age, even a small private beach of its own. But the beach was on the sound, where the water lapped gently against the shore, and my mother could see my crushing disappointment that first day. I'd been imagining huge waves that would toss me ass-over-teakettle in the surf. Whereas *this* would be like swimming in nearby Caroga Lake—the kiddie pool when I was desperate for the deep end. Though we'd already investigated the matter thoroughly at the front desk, that night my mother inquired, in a voice loud enough for people at adjacent tables to hear, what our waitress could tell us about public transportation to the other side of the island, where some real waves might be waiting for me. "Really?" she said, mock incredulous, when informed that there were neither buses nor trolleys. "None?" Next she inquired about taxis and was told that, yes, there were taxis, but to have one come all the way out-island from Vineyard Haven or Edgartown would be expensive, and then of course we'd have to prearrange for another to pick us up and bring us back to the resort. Bicycles, then? Yes, the resort did have bicycles we were welcome to use, but the nearest public surf beach was several miles away, and we'd be loaded down with beach stuff. Each revelation elicited in my mother an even deeper incredulity. "But what do people *do*?" she asked, the picture of innocence. Well, people who stayed out here generally brought their cars over on the ferry. "Oh," she said, crestfallen. "I wish we'd known." As if we owned a car.

It was at this point that a couple seated nearby introduced themselves and offered to take us to a surf beach the next day, just as my mother had been hoping all along. I could tell she'd been prepared to keep the uncomfortable conversation with the waitress going as long as need be, until someone came to our aid, but now someone had. "Of course we'll pay you," she told the couple. We wouldn't dream of imposing, and we weren't the kind of people who expected favors from complete strangers. But they said no, that was okay, they were going any-way. Before long, once it was common knowledge that we were stranded there, offers of assistance began to pour in. One rainy afternoon we were taken into Edgartown for shopping and a break from the resort's dining room, and midweek we rode along with a family to a makeshift theater in Chilmark, where an old western was projected onto a plain white wall by a projector that chewed up chunks of film, causing not just delays but gaps in the narrative, the last occurring in the final reel where, after the film was spliced, half the cast lay wounded or dead in the dirt at the O.K. Corral. By the end of the week we'd become the shared responsibility of the resort's other guests, who must have been thrilled to see us leave. "Weren't people *nice* there?" my mother said dreamily when we were back on the ferry, watching the island recede behind us like an illusion. "And punctual," she added, because everybody who promised to take us somewhere not only did so but even showed up at the agreed-upon time. "Some different, huh?"

At home we generally relied on my aunt and uncle to take us places, like the lake on weekends for picnics or special trips to Frontier Town or Fort Ticonderoga. Unlike the people who'd chauffeured us on Martha's Vineyard, they showed up when it suited them. "Why tell us ten?" my mother would say, pacing like a tiger in my grandparents' living room at 10:45, our beach stuff piled up outside on the front porch. "If you mean eleven, why not *say* eleven?"

"I'm sure they meant ten," my grandmother would say. "It's just taking them a little longer."

My aunt, of course, had to rustle all my cousins, as well as prepare the food and together with my uncle load everything into the back of the big wood-trimmed station wagons he favored. Absolved of cooking because she worked all week, my mother usually contributed Cokes and chips, which worked out to her advantage, because she disapproved of the off-brand sodas and snacks my uncle would buy if left to his own miserly devices. The longer we waited, the worse it got, until my grandfather left the room, refusing to listen. "I swear to God," she'd exclaim, "if we go to Green's after all this, I'm going to scream." Which beach we went to was always another bone of contention. My uncle preferred Green's, which was closer to town and had dozens of picnic tables interspersed on the grassy field that ran down to within a few feet of the water. There was no quick drop-off, which meant that we kids could play safely. "At Green's we ain't got to watch 'em every damn minute, Jean," he would explain when my mother complained about the little patch of sand that was always so wet you couldn't even put a blanket down. "Lay your blanket on the grass like everybody else," her brother-in-law told her. "Y'ain't gotta have sand to lie down."

My mother maintained that indeed you did need sand for a real picnic, that it was no day at the beach without a beach, that if you wanted to lie on grass you could throw a blanket down on your own backyard. "So, do that next time," my uncle, finally fed up, would tell her, winking at us kids and causing a fit of giggles. It was my aunt, I was pretty sure, who always insisted we be invited along. To her husband's way of thinking, *his* family was going in *his* car to the beach of *his* choice, and my mother and I were simply hitching a ride. My mother's logic was different. If you contributed gas money, you had certain rights, and hers were being violated every single Sunday. At the end of the day when we were dropped off on Helwig Street, she'd still be on the warpath. "Green's again," she'd tell my grandparents, clearly hoping they'd share her indignation. Instead they'd turn to me and ask if I had a good time, and I'd make the mistake of saying I had, because I loved Green's and its great expanse of grass where you could play Wiffle ball or badminton with the other kids. Better yet, there was no lifeguard, so my uncle, whose specialty was horseplay, could toss my cousin Greg and me, squealing, high into the air, somersaulting into the warm lake. I knew I wasn't supposed to like Green's, but I could never contain my enthusiasm when I described what fun we'd had, and my mother, disgusted, would clomp up the back stairs to our flat, betrayed yet again by everyone from whom she deserved some sympathy. "Whoever said beggars can't be choosers," my grandfather would remark when she was out of earshot, "never met your mother."

I HAVE TO remind myself of how young she still was back then. Not long after her death, when we were going through her things, my wife and I came across a full-page photo of her in a glossy magazine published by GE. Actually, it's a picture of their vaunted mainframe computer, but my mother's standing in front of it, looking a bit like a Fifties version of a TV game-show hostess about to tell the contestants what they'll win. Still in her thirties, she was slender and graceful, balanced expertly on high heels, her hair styled, her skirt flatteringly tailored. We showed the photo to Emily and Kate when they came home for the holidays. "Now *that*," Kate said, showing it to her new husband, "is one stylish woman."

And she was. My mother took great pains and great pride in her appearance and the contrast she offered to the slatternly, dumpy women who did shift work in Gloversville sweatshops. They dressed in cheap slacks and garish, mismatched blouses pulled from tangles of clothing mounded in the huge bins of discount stores. For them my mother felt pity that sometimes manifested itself as condescension, though she at least gave such women points for getting out of the house. She saved her real contempt for "homemakers" like the ones so popular on TV, perky, vapid wives with dull, reliable husbands and not a worry in the world. Sometimes, when my grandmother attempted to "interfere," she also got lumped into this reviled category, though God knows she was no stranger to money worries and would have looked for a job herself if she hadn't been married to a man who would've considered this an indictment of his abilities as a provider. Back then my aunt was also a homemaker, but she was raising five kids, and even my mother had to give her a pass for not having a real job. Still, she thought her sister's good fortune in having a hardworking husband who didn't drink or gamble made her one of the world's innocents, because she didn't have to face things alone, the inescapable consequence of which, of course, was dependence. And when these women's husbands brought home their paychecks and decided how the money would be spent, they had little choice but to accept their lot. They had nothing that the world needed, or nothing, at least, that it was willing to pay a living wage for. If you were a woman who'd never held a responsible job, if you didn't bring home your own paycheck at the end of the week and deposit it into an account with your own name on it, you had no right to criticize or interfere in the lives of those who did. Indeed, you had no opinions worth listening to. In the GE photograph my mother looks both old-fashioned and modern, both of her time and oddly outside of it, a strange mix of stubborn confidence and acute anxiety.

But there was another reason my mother took such ferocious pride in her personal appearance. Her marriage had failed, and having a kid in tow made things even more challenging, but she was still hopeful of finding romance. She'd always loved men and knew they found her not only attractive but likable as all get-out. She could tell a joke and take one, and she liked sports and had a good head for booze. She didn't giggle demurely like girls who were stupid or pretending to be. She presented herself as a woman seeking a mate more than a husband, as a Nora Charles searching for her Nick, except instead of having a yippy little dog for a companion, she had me. There must surely have been times she'd have liked to trade me in for a dog, because I could be as nervous and demanding as Asta and far less faithful. Worse, if allowed, I was just as willing to steal a scene.

Of course she had exactly zero interest in Gloversville men. The ones her own age she knew from high school, and there wasn't a Nick Charles in the lot. More to her taste were the guys who passed through the computer room at GE, or the kind of men who'd stopped by our table on Martha's Vineyard, men of the world who had manners and, even if they didn't major in repartee like William Powell, at least knew enough to hold the door for a lady instead of barging right on through. Many of the "fellas" who interested her had been in the service, and she was at ease with them, having been a camp follower until my father shipped overseas. After the war they'd taken full advantage of the GI Bill, as her husband had not, and now they were starting to get ahead. They dressed well and drove T-Birds and Caddies. Some took her out for lunch in Schenectady; others who were stuck there over the weekend were willing to hop on the Thruway and drive to Gloversville on a Saturday night. At this point she was legally separated but not yet divorced, and dating was one of many sources of discord between her and my grandparents, who might have suspected, despite my mother's protestations to the contrary, that some of her dates had wedding rings in their pockets. They thought she should think of me first, because Gloversville was a small town where people loved to gossip. Also, my father would cause a scene if he found out.

Which he invariably did. It was like he had a mole in the house. My mother didn't go out on dates all that often, but every time she did he'd telephone, wanting to know if this new guy understood she was a married woman. He'd ask where they were going to dinner. Maybe he'd stop by and buy them a drink. Introduce himself. Maybe he and this new guy would hit it off.

"We're separated," my mother would remind him.

"You're still my wife," he'd remind her back. "And I'm still our son's father, too."

"What's the matter? Forget his name?"

Often I'd awake the morning after one of my mother's dates vaguely aware that there'd been trouble in the night, shouting out in the street, maybe, or my mother calling downstairs, telling my grandparents that he was gone and for them to go back to sleep. Such confrontations were pretty rare, though, because they required focus and steadfast purpose on my father's part, and he famously lacked both. He'd have liked nothing better than to ambush my mother and her date at the restaurant, but apparently whoever tipped him off that his wife was stepping out didn't know where. There were no good restaurants in Gloversville itself, but too many in the surrounding area to stake out. Better to catch them later when the guy brought her home. Here this dumb bastard would be thinking maybe she'd invite him in, and instead—surprise!—there he'd be, waiting. Meanwhile, to pass the time, he'd find a card game. That was where things would invariably get away from him. He'd remember to check his watch at first, but then would get involved in the game and forget about it. Either the cards would be falling right at about the time my mother and her date would be returning, and he wouldn't want to kill his luck by cashing out, or he'd be a couple hundred bucks down and unwilling to leave until he won at least some of it back. Nor did it fail to occur to him that if he left he'd have to sit in a borrowed car up the block from my grandparents' house for who knew how long. What the hell, maybe he'd play one more hand and let the cards decide. If he won, he'd stay; if he lost, he'd drive over to Helwig Street and see what was what and what could be done about it. Except by then it would register that he'd probably waited too long: if she was already home, he'd be waiting in the dark, cold street for nothing. The next time he looked at his watch, when the game was breaking up, it was four in the morning, and the man who'd taken my mother out was back in Schenectady asleep in his hotel. My mother would be asleep, too, but sometimes he'd visit Helwig Street anyway before going home. There he'd stand beneath her bedroom window, hollering up to inquire if she'd had a good time.

Such was my mother's independence at age thirty. She was free, but couldn't do as she pleased. Though she could go wherever she liked, she had no way of getting there. She had her own money, but it ran out before she could spend it on anything she really wanted. Men liked her—how she looked and danced and laughed—and under different circumstances she would've had no great difficulty finding someone. But the circumstances weren't different; they were always the same. The men she liked were mostly passing through and often lost interest once they were introduced to me or to my tight-lipped grandparents or to Gloversville itself. Some of them probably came from places that were pretty similar, but after the war they were done with these backwater burgs.

Even to my mother, her hard-won autonomy must at times have resembled a cage. Still, it was a cage of her own design, different from and superior to the one my father and her parents and Gloversville itself would have put her in if she'd allowed them to. In retrospect what astonishes me is the courage she must have summoned in order to imagine—by working in Schenectady, by having her own checking account, by going out on the occasional date—that she was outside the cage she so clearly was trapped in. She had to muster that tough imagining day after day, year after year, with all of life's realities bearing down on her relentlessly, insinuating, as self-doubts always do, that the sensible thing would be to give up. And with no one to talk to about any of this but a boy.

What kept her going? Stubbornness? Vanity? My mother did love mirrors, often practicing in front of them. But I came to understand that this vanity had its origins in fear and, counterintuitively, intense empathy. One of her favorite family stories was of a particular Easter during the Depression. My grandfather had somehow managed to scrape together enough money to buy her and her sister new outfits, and he made a great fuss about how beautiful they were, picking each of them up and twirling them in the air above his head, assuring them they'd be the prettiest girls at Easter Mass. When he finally set them down, he took his wife in his arms and said, "And you look beautiful, too," though that spring there wasn't enough money to buy her anything new. My mother was on morphine the last time she shared this story with me. It was clear that the memory still haunted her, in part, I suspect, because it effortlessly yielded two irreconcilable morals. I don't think she ever doubted how much her father loved her mother, or that he thought she was beautiful, no matter how threadbare the dress she was wearing. Seen as a parable of love versus material goods, love wins hands-down. But I think to my mother the story also suggested, as it would to so many who'd weathered the Dirty Thirties, that in this world there's never enough to go around. Love couldn't stretch two new outfits into three, or fill three hungry bellies with food for two. If you depended on a man, even one who loved you, you could end up in church with people staring with pity at your moth-eaten clothes. And who knew? Maybe love followed the same laws, and there wasn't enough of that to go around either.

For whatever reason, or combination of reasons, I think my mother made up her mind never to be that woman without something pretty to wear. There was no character in literature or film with whom she identified more completely than Scarlett O'Hara (speaking of brave, ferocious, stubborn vanity), and her favorite scene in *Gone With the Wind* was when Scarlett, penniless and hungry, makes a gown out of Tara's velvet drapes. In the last few months of my mother's life, her Easter story seemed to morph on her, as if after so many tellings its true meaning was only now coming clear to her. She kept trying and failing to describe the exact expression on her mother's face when her father told her that she, too, was beautiful. I wasn't there, of course. I didn't see it. But I knew my grandmother, and I know her expression would have contained both love and understanding. But having seen photographs of her as a young mother, I also know what those Depression years, so full of want and fear, had done to her handsome features.

And so I wouldn't be surprised if what my mother saw on her face was defeat.

AND THERE WAS one more reason—this one less personal—my mother kept soldiering forward when reason dictated simply giving up: those were optimistic times. Like the men she occasionally dated, the postwar nation was thriving. Servicemen had returned triumphant, and when the partying stopped they parlayed their brand-new GI Bill degrees, their new skills, their hard-earned worldly experience and brimming confidence into houses in the suburbs and two-car garages. When JFK became president, it seemed to many, including my mother, that the country had turned a corner, that barriers excluding people like her were finally coming down. Opportunities seemed to be everywhere. To be left behind when everyone around you was getting ahead, she thought, you'd have to be stupid or lazy—or married to Jimmy Russo and living in Fulton County (which JFK had not carried). My mother wasn't stupid, and she wasn't lazy, and she'd separated from my father, so . . .

So. "You," she told me throughout high school, "are getting out of Gloversville."

I was a decent student, but uneven and undisciplined, far too interested in girls and having a good time to really excel. I got excited about all sorts of things, then invariably lost interest when I discovered they were difficult and there was no one to help guide me through their intricacies. My mother had told me for as long as I could remember that I could be anything I wanted to be, and I took this to mean, despite a complete lack of evidence, that I was gifted. While my teachers tried their best to offer a counterbalancing view, I was having none of it. Senior year, though, I did well enough on my Regents Exams to qualify for significant financial assistance to any college in New York. But I'd also found out that the universities out west were much cheaper. If I lit out for the territories, the first year would be rough because I'd have to pay out-of-state tuition, but by the second I'd have established residency, and it would cost less to go to the University of Arizona without financial aid than to SUNY with a scholarship. I expected my mother to put up stiff resistance to this plan; after all, I'd be twenty-five hundred miles away and her mantra had always been that we were a team, that as long as we had each other, we'd be able to manage. So I should have been suspicious when she didn't object to my heading west. But even if I'd twigged to the possibility that she was up to something, I never would've grasped the obvious inference, and it was years before it occurred to me that maybe the westward-ho notion hadn't been mine at all, that she'd steadily been dropping hints—for example, that the best place to study archaeology, my current interest, was the Desert Southwest—and that I'd dutifully been lapping them up. Nor did she object when, in spring of my senior year, I announced I wanted to buy a car.

The reason she didn't, of course, was that we'd need one. Because she was coming with me.

A Good Talking-To

I N THE SPRING of 1967 I bought a big, hulking 1960 Ford Galaxie, the first car ever to sit at the curb of 36 Helwig Street. Everything about it—exterior, dashboard, vinyl upholstery—was a dull, battleship gray, so my friends immediately christened it the Gray Death. It's hard to imagine the car had ever been shiny, even in the showroom, but there was no rust on it, which in upstate New York was remarkable. Still, cars didn't get much more uncool, and to make matters worse the Death, with its small V-6 engine, was seriously underpowered. I would own worse cars, but never another in which you could slam the accelerator to the floor and nothing, absolutely nothing, would happen. You simply couldn't express urgency to the fucking thing. Getting on the Thruway at Fultonville, you wouldn't get up to the speed limit until Amsterdam, seven miles down the road.

For our trip across country I hitched a U-Haul to the rear bumper, and into this we crammed my mother's books, our clothes, television, kitchen stuff, and other miscellaneous items she couldn't bear to part with. Her plan was to find a furnished apartment in Phoenix, where General Electric had a branch office. She admitted to being a little worried she might not make quite as much money there as she did in Schenectady, but we had distant relatives who lived in Scottsdale, and they claimed that the cost of living was much lower, so hopefully the two would cancel each other out. Later, after she got established, my mother could move into an unfurnished place and have the bulk of our furniture shipped out from Gloversville. She kept this scheme hidden from her parents as long as possible, knowing they'd consider it rash and do everything in their power to dissuade her, as indeed they did. Phoenix was a big city, they pointed out, in which she didn't know a soul. Did she have any idea what rents there were like? Where was that kind of money going to come from? In nine months, tops, she'd be broke, and then what would she do? How would she even get back home? My grandfather's emphysema had progressed to the point where he couldn't work anymore, and his meager pension and retirement barely covered their monthly needs. Eventually my mother would discover her mistake and rely on them to rescue her, like she always did. Did she understand that now they simply couldn't manage to?

But all of this was assuming we'd make it there in the first place. Our whole trip, according to my grandfather, was under-funded, my mother's calculations based on wishful thinking.

Gas. Motels. Food. Auto repairs. At the wheel of our unsafe
car was someone who'd had his license only a few months,
and my mother couldn't even spell me at the wheel. Did she
understand that what she was proposing wasn't just financial
folly but also dangerous, potentially even tragic? To all this, my
mother responded that she wasn't a child and didn't appreciate being treated like one, adding for good measure that their
refusal to treat her like an adult was one of the reasons she
was leaving. She'd carefully budgeted the trip according to the
recommendations of AAA, which had even mapped out our
route. And she *had* planned for the unexpected, laying aside
an emergency fund we could dip into if we needed to. She had
every confidence in my driving ability. We would go slow. We
would be safe as houses.

In the weeks before our departure 36 Helwig Street, the
sanctuary of my childhood, became a battleground, a place of
bitter recrimination and slamming doors. The only thing that
kept the arguments from escalating was that my grandfather
didn't have the breath, and after a few minutes he'd have to
get up from the kitchen table, go into the living room, and
hook himself up to the oxygen tank standing sentry behind
his armchair. Even my mother could see what the strife was
doing to him, and so a terrible silence descended that was even
worse. No matter where I happened to be, upstairs or down, I
was behind enemy lines and chose, coward that I was, to stay
away as much as possible. It was a summer of farewell parties, of the Doors advising us to break on through to the other
side, of freedom. One day, though, I came home and found my

grandfather sleeping in his chair, his chest heaving violently up and down, as it often did now, awake or asleep. I thought my mother was up in our apartment, but went into the kitchen and she was sitting there with my grandmother, who reached across the table and took her hand. The gesture surprised me, because they seldom touched or talked intimately. "Jean," she said, and waited until my mother met her eye. "This trip. You're in no *condition*."

I could have been wrong, but I got the distinct impression that my mother might be about to concede something important, perhaps a fear, or a misgiving, but she looked up, saw me, and quickly withdrew her hand, leaving me to wonder how that moment would have played out if I'd come home a few minutes later. It might have been my first intimation of how whole lives—maybe even my own—could pivot on such perfectly poised moments of stillness.

MY MOTHER'S "CONDITION." This was something the whole family seemed aware of, but no one talked about it. One word, *nerves,* was evidently deemed sufficient to describe, categorize, stigmatize, and dismiss it. As a child I remember being frightened of whatever was wrong with my mother because it seemed at once serious and, for the most part, without visible symptoms. Nor, apparently, was there anything to be done about it. I wondered anxiously if I might one day come down with nerves, but from what I could gather men didn't get them. Certain women, my mother among them, seemingly had more than their share, and if they became too nervous they could even have something called a breakdown. This had happened to other women in my grandmother's family and more recently to my uncle's mother, though she wasn't a blood relation. The idea of my own mother suffering one of these nervous breakdowns was terrifying to me, because then she wouldn't be living with us on Helwig Street but rather in some kind of hospital. Some suffering women were given electroshock treatments, after which they weren't nervous anymore, or aware of their surroundings or that it was Tuesday. *Nervous Breakdown.* The phrase haunted my childhood, in part because it could happen to my mother, but also because I came to understand that I might be its cause. Her health was in *my* hands. Other kids were good because they didn't want to get punished if they misbehaved; I was good because I feared that if I misbehaved it was my mother who'd be punished.

But here's the thing about conditions, especially pervasive, largely asymptomatic ones: over time, when the worst doesn't happen, they gradually lose their power to terrify. They simply become part of the landscape—as real as anything else, but also as ordinary. I observed that my mother's nerves were cyclical, like the moon, waxing and waning, and by paying attention, I could tell where we were in the cycle. Which in turn suggested that maybe her health *wasn't* in my hands, at least not entirely. True, it was in my power to make things worse, a lot worse, if I chose to, but I couldn't make them much better. There were other forces at work, as powerful and inexorable and impersonal as gravity, as regular and predictable as the tides. And most of the time she seemed fine. At some previous low point she'd confessed to our family doctor that the stress of being a single mother and, in addition, working full-time sometimes made her awfully nervous, and he immediately prescribed a low dose of phenobarbital. Over the years these dosages incrementally increased, and in due course barbiturates gave way to newer drugs like Valium. Afraid of becoming addicted, she cut pills in half when she was doing well, but then upped the dosage when she "needed help." Eventually she developed a tremor in her hands, though it was never clear to me whether this was due to stress or the medication she was taking to alleviate it. Most of the time her condition was part and parcel of our lives, a subtext that under the right circumstances might become a text.

And, on occasion, a screeching ALL CAPS hypertext, a gale of fury and paranoia and accusation and heartbreaking despair. "I can't *take* it anymore!" she'd scream. "Doesn't anybody under*stand*? I can't *take* it!" Sometimes these episodes had specific triggers—a raise or bonus at work that she expected but that didn't come through, or I'd get into some kind of trouble at school, or a GE man she was dating would break things off, or she'd be blindsided by some unanticipated expense. But more often what she couldn't take anymore was vague, almost global. She felt it as a weight whose source might be too much responsibility or accumulated disappointment or mounting despair. Whatever was wrong or out of balance would grow slowly until suddenly everything in the world was wrong, and utter panic would ensue. Wild eyed, she'd often fix her gaze on me and ask unanswerable questions: "Don't I deserve a *life*? Am I so different from everyone else? Don't I deserve what other people have?" As a boy what scared me the most about such questions wasn't that I had none of the answers my mother so desperately sought. No, it was that it didn't seem possible for these questions to be asked without consequence. What would my mother *do* if I couldn't manage to console her? "Doesn't anyone understand that things have to *change*?" she'd wail. "That something will *happen* to me if they don't?"

By the time I was in high school, though, this much had become clear: in fact, nothing was going to happen. At least nothing as dramatic as her hysterical questions implied. Because the result was the same every time she had one of these meltdowns. The morning after she'd appear at the break-fast table, so exhausted by what she'd been through that she could barely lift the coffee cup, but her emotional equilibrium for the most part restored. "Ah, Ricko-Mio," she sighed, using her pet name for me. "Don't worry. Everything's going to be fine." She'd give my hand a reassuring pat. "Last night, after you went to bed, I gave myself a good talking-to."

That phrase always gave me the willies, because it squared with nothing in my experience. As a boy I'd had a condition of my own, a terrible temper, and knew firsthand what a near-total loss of control felt like. My mother's meltdowns could be scary, but at least they were analogous to something I myself had experienced. But I'd never given myself a good talking-to. For that to happen there would have to be two of me, and I was always one, even when unhinged. I understood that my mother's phrase could be interpreted as a figure of speech, though I also suspected that fundamentally it wasn't. She wasn't thinking things through more calmly or considering things from a new angle due to conscience, rituals I was conscious of and familiar with from a fairly young age. But I'd never given myself a dressing-down. There was simply no other me to assume the talked-to position. If I deserved a lecture, there was no me to give it; if I had one to impart, neither was there another me to receive it. Somehow, my mother was able to do that. More bizarrely still, it worked.

It just didn't last.

THE CONFLICT BETWEEN my mother and grandparents came to a head in the week before we were scheduled to leave. Given that our future well-being, if not our very lives, was being wagered on an ill-conceived cross-country journey, their final battle was over something relatively insignificant: my mother's furniture, the stuff we weren't taking with us in the U-Haul and that she couldn't afford to put in storage. She wanted to store it in Helwig Street's small, dark, dank basement, but my grandfather said there was too little space, that with all that furniture stacked down there, it would be hard to get at the furnace, should it need servicing. But more likely he hoped that when it came down to selling all her worldly goods for what little they'd bring, my mother would finally see the folly of the whole enterprise and come to her senses. Instead, she assured them that this was the last time she'd *ever* ask them for *anything* and promptly called a man who dealt in used furniture. He came to the house, looked everything over critically, and concluded that he'd be doing her a favor, really, just to haul it away. There wasn't much of a market for such old-fashioned stuff, he claimed, and a lot of the pieces sported dark cigarette burns, courtesy of my father, who couldn't be bothered to use an ashtray and who managed, despite his brief tenure on Helwig Street, to leave his mark on flat surfaces in every room.

By the time we got to Ohio, naturally, she'd decided the guy was a highway robber. She'd waited too long to get a second appraisal, and he'd known we didn't have time to haggle and would take whatever he offered, no matter how unfair it was. No doubt he'd spent a leisurely morning sanding the burns off the arms of our furniture, which was *not* old-fashioned but classic, timeless. By now he'd applied a coat of polyurethane and was selling it for three times what he paid us. Ten times, probably. And this was money we could use, she admitted, because of course by Ohio she knew that my grandfather had been right. Everything *was* costing more than she'd budgeted, and she now feared we might have to dip into the emergency fund, which she at last revealed was my college money. All because of a thief. "Gloversville," she muttered, shaking her head in disgust. How lucky we were to finally be shut of such an awful, awful place.

WE WERE SCARED, if not nearly as scared as we should have been. It was beyond lunatic to set out in a vehicle as dubious as the Gray Death with a novice at the wheel, on a twenty-five-hundred-mile journey. In the weeks before our departure, I'd gotten on the Thruway a few times to get used to interstate driving, but usually got off again at the next exit and returned home. I knew we were budgeted, as indeed we always were, right down to the last nickel, and it seemed a waste of time and gas to drive to Amsterdam, pay my toll, and then turn around and drive back. Those short trial runs weren't a waste, though. I at least got a sense of how much faster everybody else would be going, that even eighteen-wheelers were going to blow by me like I was standing still, and that even a vehicle as sluggish and heavy as the Galaxie could be tugged into their wake. I also learned to stay in the right-hand lane and to disregard the pissed-off expressions of impatient drivers who'd get trapped behind me, then roar past with horns blaring and middle fingers erect. What that relatively benign stretch of Thruway could not prepare me for, of course, was the white-knuckle traffic in and around major cities, nor for the trailer I'd be towing.

Nor could I imagine that while my plan to poke along in the right lane would work well enough most of the time, I'd eventually have to change lanes and learn on the fly how much space between cars to allow for both the Death and the trailer. Our first day on the road I must've nearly caused a half-dozen accidents, and the drivers I imperiled by unsafe lane changes, their red faces contorted with rage in my side-view mirrors, retaliated by laying on their horns before swerving in front of me to see how I liked it. One man I cut off pulled alongside and powered down his window to yell at me, but then didn't. I don't know if it was my age and obvious inexperience or my bewildered-looking passenger, but the righteous fury instantly drained out of his face, and I could read his thoughts clearly. Whoever we were and wherever we were going, we weren't going to make it. "What's wrong with all these people?" my mother kept wondering. "Why's everybody so *mad* at us?" I didn't have the heart to explain what I was only just coming to understand myself: we were a genuine menace.

On the morning of the second day, studying the course AAA had charted for us, she said, "I don't know why they want us to go around all these cities. The road we're on goes straight through. Why burn all that extra gas?" Her question got answered that afternoon in Indiana when we decided to ignore AAA's advice to loop around Indianapolis. Immediately we found ourselves locked in a sea of angry city commuters, and to my complete surprise the right-hand lane was no longer ideal, because it would end abruptly, forcing us to exit—or, rather, another driver would have. I, however, had no intention of getting off for the simple reason that we didn't want to. Putting on my left-turn blinker, I simply held my course, in effect creating my own lane, until one of the drivers in the lane I was determined to merge with, fearing death or dismemberment, let me in. "What a *good* driver you're becoming," my mother said every time we didn't have a wreck, and I couldn't tell if she was trying to bolster my confidence or actually meant it.

What we worried about even more than accidents were the interstate on-ramps. The Death, underpowered to begin with and further slowed by the U-Haul, simply wasn't up to them. I'd get up the best head of steam I could and keep the accelerator pressed to the floor as I entered the ramp, but then there was nothing to do but watch the speedometer inch backward—20, 18, 15, 11—until finally our forward momentum wouldn't even register at all and the car would begin to shudder violently. "Come on, Bess," my mother would whisper, patting the metal dashboard encouragingly, terrified that we'd come to a complete halt and block the long line of cars behind us, "you can do it." (She refused to call our getaway car the Death and became irritated when I did.) All the way to Arizona, our lives were ruled by ramps. We had to get on and off the interstate several times a day, but no matter how low we were on gas, or how hungry we were, or how badly my mother needed to pee, if the exit's ramps, whether off or back on, looked too severe we kept on driving until we found one with a gentler incline. At day's end we avoided the busy exits where we'd have a choice of places to stay and eat, opting instead for more remote ones where there'd be a lone Holiday Inn that had an on-site restaurant, because once we were done for the day, there was no chance we'd be getting back in the car before morning. We parked in the farthest, darkest reaches of the motel's parking lot, taking up three or four spaces, because our one absolutely inviolable rule was to never, for any reason, put the Death in reverse. One morning early on I'd wasted a good hour trying to back out of the space we'd taken near the motel's front entrance. No one had told me that backing a trailer would be counterintuitive, and before I'd figured that out I'd jackknifed the U-Haul so completely that the two cars to my left were utterly hemmed in. We'd had to enlist the help of the desk clerk to locate and rouse from their slumbers the drivers of the two vehicles on my right so I could extricate us by means of a forward gear.

My other great concern was the temperature gauge, especially in the afternoon when the July heat was worst and the needle crept slowly up into the red danger range. Then we'd have to pull over at a rest stop and let the ticking engine cool down. When I couldn't find one in time and radiator steam began to billow from under the hood, the only solution was to pull onto the shoulder and wait for an hour in the broiling sun. What I didn't like thinking about was that we still hadn't crossed the Mississippi. What would happen when we hit the desert and the temperature soared into the hundreds? Standing there beside the interstate, wilting in the brutal heat, the steady stream of air-conditioned cars and professionally maintained trucks whizzing by and blowing angry gales of dust in our faces, we must have looked utterly forlorn. Surprisingly few people stopped to offer assistance, and those who did we quickly sent packing. Everything was fine, we told them. No, we didn't need a tow. We were just waiting a bit for the engine to cool down, and then we'd be on the road again. We didn't want complete strangers to know our true plight, or that we were losing heart with each passing mile.

I kept expecting my mother to throw in the towel. As soon as she did, I was prepared to pack it in and return home. I'd find a job and put off college until the following year. Or maybe I'd contact my father. You never could tell with him. Sometimes he'd just happen to have what you needed, and if he had the money he'd buy me a plane ticket to Arizona or help get me on a road-construction crew if he didn't. But my mother knew me as well as I knew her, so she had to know what was going through my brain, and the closest she ever came to calling it quits was to remark, at the end of one of those long, hot, dusty, scarifying days, "Ah, Ricko-Mio. *When* are we going to catch a break?" As if our problem were bad luck.

Not long after, though, our luck did change, in the Ozarks of all places, where a gas station attendant with the smallest head I'd ever seen on an adult sold us a brown canvas water bag shaped like a pancreas that he swore would solve our radiator problem. As near as I could tell from his toothless explanation, offered up as he attached the thing to the Galaxie's bug-splattered grille, the hot outside air would be cooled as it passed through the bag, the cooler air then blowing directly onto the radiator. I had my doubts, but the gadget seemed to reassure my mother, who now had only entrance and exit ramps, reverse gear, wrong turns, and running out of money before we got to Arizona to worry about. First thing each morning, and every time we stopped for gas, I refilled the bag with cool water as quickly and unobtrusively as I could, hoping no one would ask what on earth I was doing and oblige me to repeat, this time with added consonants, the pump jockey's rationale. But guess what? *The car stopped overheating.* Then, a couple days later in the Texas Panhandle, somebody actually stole the bag when we stopped for lunch. This was a blow to my mother, whose excellent opinion of people outside of Fulton County was being rubbed raw by actual experience of them, but the theft cheered me considerably, suggesting as it did that there were apparently other idiots in the world. They weren't all in our car. Over the next several days, though, every time we stopped for gas in the parched southwestern desert, my mother inquired of the attendant whether they sold those great water bags, the ones you attached to the grille to keep car radiators cool. Even after she patiently described the bag's size and shape and color, nobody seemed to know what she was talking about. Apparently you could buy them only in Missouri from congenital nitwits.

MY MOTHER'S NEW JOB at the General Electric plant in Phoenix had always sounded a little vague to me. When I asked what she'd be doing there, if there'd be any correlation between her new duties and the work she'd done in the computer room in Schenectady, or how much of a pay cut she was taking, she said she'd find out all that when we arrived. The main thing, she added, was that the people were nice. Her new boss was somebody she knew, sort of, having talked with him on the phone, off and on, for years, and he was always saying how great it would be if she came out west. She spoke of him in the same tone of voice she used to describe the men she occasionally dated at GE, which might be why I never pressed her for details. Maybe they'd met in Schenectady. Maybe this was one of the guys who'd taken her out for lunch. I didn't want to know, that's for sure. Whatever her reasoning, she seemed confident that any salary or tenure she lost as a result of the move, she would quickly be able to make up. After all, the Schenectady plant was GE's flagship, and in lowly Phoenix she'd surely be recognized as someone who knew how things were done in the big leagues. She just hoped she could start work immediately because, well, the trip *had* cost more than she'd planned, and she didn't want to tap the emergency fund any more than she absolutely had to. Right around the corner there'd be first and last month's rent on her new apartment, and when you went grocery shopping that first time it was always extra expensive because you needed to get everything: salt, pepper, a two-pound bag of flour, wax paper, you name it. And she'd have to pay for her ride to work, just as she'd always done.

Nor was it just money that was in short supply. Time was also of our particular essence. In a couple weeks I'd be heading to Tucson to register for my fall semester classes and check into my dorm. My mother was a list maker, and the to-do items on the list she'd started back in Gloversville and updated periodically during our journey—find an apartment she could afford, move in, return the U-Haul and collect the deposit, open a bank account, set up phone and utilities, locate a grocery store within walking distance, find a new doctor—all had to be checked off before I headed south in the car.

As my mother obsessed about all these tasks, I became increasingly apprehensive, not so much because the list was long and time was short, but because she herself seemed so keyed up. After all, our harrowing journey was behind us.

Against all odds—we didn't even know enough to calculate them when we left Helwig Street—we'd somehow made it. The Gray Death hadn't killed us, and neither, miraculously, had I. We'd done the hard part, hadn't we? Once we got close to Phoenix, my mother had contacted our relatives, and they'd offered to let us stay with them for a few days until we settled in, and they proved a wealth of information about the area. Sure, there was a lot left to do, but unlike the journey itself none of it was likely to kill us. So, why was my mother behaving as if the tough part was only now beginning? The reason was that she hadn't written down on any list the most important thing she had to do: *Find A Job*.

In fairness, some part of her thought she had one. Not in the sense that an actual job had been offered and she'd accepted it, or that there'd been any discussion of things like salary or hours or a start date, and certainly not in the sense that there were any supporting documents. More like, *If you're ever out this way, look us up.* Or, *We could sure use somebody like you out here.* Her having a job there was essentially a reasonable conjecture, a deduction based on available data. Telling my grandparents that she had a job in Arizona wasn't a lie, exactly. It wasn't that she didn't have a job, only that she didn't have one *yet*. A matter of semantics, surely. She was confident about both her marketable skills and her considerable experience, and that when she presented herself to the man with whom she'd chatted so pleasantly on the phone, he'd recognize her value and find something for her. Having spent his entire working life in Gloversville's skin mills, my grandfather couldn't be expected to understand how things worked out in the wider world, in a big company like General Electric. GE people looked out for one another.

But mostly I think my mother believed she had that job in Phoenix because she needed it so badly. Because if she didn't have it, then doing what we'd just done was beyond folly. Because without a job waiting for her out west, when I went off to college she'd be left behind on Helwig Street. Because she was in her mid-forties now and still an attractive woman, but for how much longer? And more to the point, how long was any person with hopes and dreams expected to remain in a cage, without hope, without a life to call her own? She had the job in Phoenix because without it she was finished. Because for my sake she'd stuck it out in Gloversville as long as she could, and she couldn't stand it a moment longer. She just couldn't. And so she had a job.

THE GE FACILITY WAS located on the other side of Phoenix, even then, in 1967, an obscenity of urban sprawl. It was more of an outpost than anything, and I could see my mother's face fall when she saw how small it was, about the size of an automobile dealership. She'd dressed with great care that morning, but it was already close to a hundred degrees out, and in the hour it had taken us to drive there her hair and clothes were limp. Even more discouraging were the people emerging from and entering the facility, the women dressed in slacks and casual tops and sneakers, the men in jeans and shirts with snaps instead of buttons. A few even wore cowboy hats. One of these pointed my mother to an office door into which she disappeared on her high heels. I found a shady spot, expecting to roast there awhile in the punishing heat, but less than five minutes later she returned. The man who'd encouraged her to come by if she was ever in the area hadn't worked there for a year. In his place was a woman who informed my mother that not only were there no openings but also none were anticipated. Theirs was a very small operation, and almost everyone who worked there had done so forever. If she'd had such a good job in Schenectady, why did she leave it?

For a few minutes we just sat in the car and let the blazing desert sun bake us. I saw my mother's hands were shaking. I was about to ask what she meant to do now, when she said, "How can anyone even *think* in heat like this?"

We went to an air-conditioned coffee shop and sat in a window booth, our wet clothes sticking to the vinyl cushions. Outside, the heat shimmered in waves off the pavement. Everything was singed brown, even the weeds pushing up through cracks in the sidewalks. "What an awful, awful place," my mother remarked, more to herself than me. "All that way we came."

I was inclined to agree, but pointed out that we'd been in Phoenix less than twenty-four hours, perhaps not long enough to pass judgment.

"I can tell you one thing," she said, finally turning to face me, and there was something wild in her eyes, something so desperate it bordered on rabid. I'd seen it, or something like it, a few times before, usually when she was at wit's end and instead of helping I, her only ally, did or said something to make things even worse. At such times it seemed to occur to her that maybe I'd been enlisted in the swelling ranks of those determined to thwart her. Who knew? Maybe I'd always been against her. "I can tell you one thing," she repeated, challenging me to disagree. "I'm not going back."

EVENTUALLY SHE DID, of course, just as my grandparents had foretold, but by then a lot had happened, some of it predictable but mostly not, at least not by me. Sitting across from my mother in that Phoenix coffee shop, I couldn't even have predicted the next two weeks, at the end of which she and I would once again put the Gray Death on the road, minus the U-Haul this time, for the relatively short trip down to Tucson, where over the next decade, I would complete both an undergraduate and several graduate degrees, and where I would meet a girl named Barbara whom I had the good sense to fall in love with and, once I'd overruled her better judgment, marry. In Tucson I would become a man, a husband, a scholar, a father, and a writer.

In the summer of 1967, however, I was still a boy and my mother's son, and the University of Arizona larger and more populous than my hometown. I wasn't the boy who'd left Gloversville a month earlier, though. Nor, I think, was my mother the same woman. We'd become seasoned, fearless travelers and found first the U of A and then the dorm to which I'd been assigned (Apache Hall, I still remember), without difficulty or incident. There I met my roommate, an Arizonan who'd grown up in a small, godforsaken mining town he seemed proud of as only a small-town boy can be. To me, it sounded like the local equivalent of an upstate New York mill town. My mother garrulously told him all about where we were from, and from her description you never would've guessed that for her Gloversville held anything but the fondest of memories. Later, the kid told me he thought she was cool. In fact, motherwise, I'd lucked out. Definitely. He'd have continued in this vein, I suspect, if I hadn't cut him off.

We were broke, of course, so that night my mother and I ate dinner at a chain coffee shop near the interstate, a dead ringer for the one in Phoenix we'd retreated to after she learned she wouldn't be working for GE anymore. There was a pay phone outside, so we called my grandparents to let them know that this final leg of our journey had been successfully completed and I was registered for all my classes, which would begin next week. I gave them the number of the phone at the end of the hall in my dorm so they could reach me if they needed to. And of course they had my mother's new number in Phoenix. "How *good* they were to us," she said over dinner, and I understood from this that she'd begun the process of forgetting those last terrible weeks on Helwig Street. Hearing my grandfather struggle for breath on the telephone brought home to her not just how much she loved him but how much she'd depended on him, and her remark about how good they'd been to us was really about the whole of the last eighteen years.

"I don't know what we would've done without them," she said, as close as she'd ever come to admitting that we hadn't been wholly self-sufficient living under their roof and how secretly worried she was about losing the safety net they'd provided. "He was always my rock," she continued, her eyes brimming, "from the time I was a little girl," letting her voice fall, but not completely. "*You're* that rock now."

If it had occurred to me that she actually meant this, I'd have protested, because I didn't feel like anybody's rock, including my own. I was also acutely aware that for the last eighteen years the only rock I'd been was the one around her neck, threatening to pull her under. And if she was worried about the future, she had me for company. That afternoon I'd opened a checking account with a couple hundred dollars, money that would have to last me through the first semester, and in my pocket was a cafeteria meal ticket that would keep me from starving. I couldn't think of a single thing I had that would be of the slightest use if my mother ran into trouble. My two suitcases were full of clothes that were stylish back home but would brand me as a hated easterner out here in the desert, where the frat-boy uniform was cowboy boots, button-down oxford shirts, and jeans with button flies. I'd have all I could do not to become a figure of fun. My numerous misgivings about coming this far to study in what amounted to a foreign country must have been obvious to my mother. She might even have suspected I'd have done a straight-up swap to be enrolling back at SUNY Albany, where I'd know people and could hop on a bus and be home in Gloversville in an hour. So when my mother said that I was now her rock I assumed she was just expressing some kindly sunrise-sunset, swiftly-flow-the-years sentiment meant to buck me up in the face of new challenges.

She wasn't.

THE COFFEE-SHOP MELTDOWN in Phoenix turned out to be the nadir. Somehow my mother gathered herself, and we returned to Scottsdale, to the home of the people who were putting us up and in whose yard our detached U-Haul now sat, its ball hitch burrowing into their desert landscaping like an anteater's snout. My mother found an excuse to go straight to bed, where she slept around the clock. Bright and early the next morning, though, we set about crossing items off her revised to-do list, at the top of which she'd now written *JOB*.

The first major piece of the puzzle to fall into place was an apartment. Phoenix, a stunningly horizontal city, was even then deeply committed to both unplanned sprawl and the primacy of automobiles, policies that remain unquestioned to this day as far as I know. New apartment houses with acres of parking were springing up everywhere in an attempt to keep up with the influx of midwestern snowbirds. Their construction was shabby, but to easterners used to the grit and grime born of punishing winters they felt new and clean. Several complexes that were only half built offered a free month or two to anyone willing to sign a year's lease, and that put pressure on older, established properties to cut similar deals. My mother picked a place on Indian School Road that was reasonably close to most of what she'd need, though of course nothing was walking distance, a moot point since there were no sidewalks. Perhaps because it was so hot and gas was nineteen cents a gallon, people preferred to get in their cars even when their destination was just a block or two away.

She could've gotten by with a studio apartment, but my mother rented a one bedroom so I'd have at least a couch to crash on when I visited. She had to come up with the usual first and last month's rent, but after that her next check wasn't due until November, which seemed a long way off. To her surprise and delight, almost everybody in the complex was newly divorced and recently arrived from somewhere else, men seeming to outnumber women three to one. All of which made sense when you thought about it. In most divorces it would be the man who found himself without a roof over his head, and most of these guys wanted to put at least a few miles between themselves and the wives who'd told them to hit the bricks. Nobody seemed to have much money or to care much about it. There were a few flashy sports cars in the parking lot, but just as many beaters. In the interior courtyard was a large swimming pool with a communal grill where people congregated in the evenings after changing into bathing suits and grabbing a cold beer. On Saturdays, around midday, somebody would appear on the pool deck with a pitcher of margaritas and give a rebel yell. People would then spill out of their apartments, blinking in the bright sun like prisoners released from their cells by an invisible warden. Then the weekend festivities would begin.

It must've been pretty close to the kind of life my mother had been imagining back in Gloversville. She also must've felt like she'd arrived in the nick of time, because most of her neighbors were younger, in their thirties, but they welcomed her like the bunch of good-natured drunks they were. "New blood!" one bare-chested young fellow called up to us from the barbecue pit, his gleaming spatula raised in triumph, when we moved my mother's stuff into her second-floor apartment within hours of signing the lease. "Where you from?"

"Upstate New York," my mother called over the railing. She hadn't caught on yet that here in Arizona, hailing from back east was more likely to elicit derision than admiration.

"Well, Jean," he said, after they'd exchanged first names, "you're better off here. How do you like your burgers?" When she told him, he said to come down when we finished lugging boxes, then pointed his greasy spatula at me. "Bring your husband with you."

The next morning we dropped the trailer off at the nearest U-Haul facility where a HELP WANTED sign was taped to the cash register. "Not for here," the man behind the counter said, as if he feared my mother had designs on his job. "At the headquarters."

These were again located all the way across town, so we drove directly there, my mother having learned her lesson about dressing up for job interviews, and when she disappeared inside I again found a shady spot where I could plan, with the aid of a map of Phoenix, the rest of our day. My mother wasn't very good at sequencing the items on her to-do list. She always wanted to attend to things in the order of their importance, without taking geographical proximity and other natural progressions into account. I'd only just begun when she reappeared. "Where's that list?" she said. When I handed it to her, she crossed out *JOB*. "No kidding?" I said. No kidding. She'd been hired on the spot as a bookkeeper. The pay was shitty, but Arizona was a virulently antiunion, right-to-work state where the idea of a living wage had yet to be introduced. There were lots and lots of crappy, low-paying jobs, however, and the possibility of rapid advancement. I think what really sold her on this one, though, was that it was located straight down Indian School Road, so that even with her lousy sense of direction she wouldn't get lost. Turn right to go to work, turn left and return home. Easy as pie.

That was the other complication, naturally. My car wasn't mine anymore. "I wish there was some other way," she'd said the morning after her coffee-shop meltdown. But of course I'd seen it coming. The people we'd been staying with had explained when my mother mentioned I'd be taking the car down to Tucson that people in Phoenix didn't carpool. Or ride the bus, or take a train. If you needed to go anywhere, you climbed in your own car and you took off. If your wife needed to go somewhere, she got into *her* own car and *she* took off. You'd no more go two to a car than two to a horse. "But isn't that kind of, well . . . stupid?" I remember asking. "Welcome to Arizona," I was told.

So, since I didn't really need a car at the university anyway, we located the nearest branch of the Department of Motor

Vehicles, got my mother a learner's permit, and scheduled the written and driving exams for a week later. What we'd do if she failed either one we tried our best not to think about. With nothing but Camelback Mountain to go around and a few dry arroyos to go over, Phoenix wasn't a bad place to learn to drive. It was laid out on a grid, and its streets were wide and flat. To us, every intersection looked like every other intersection, but you could see for long distances, so it was possible to use the few landmarks that stood out to orient yourself. There was the heat, of course. Since the Death had neither air-conditioning nor power steering, we waited until late in the day for her driving lessons. For the first few evenings we practiced on quiet, residential streets and abandoned strip-mall parking lots. My mother was not a gifted student, but in her defense it must've been hard to learn such a basic skill so late in life and to be taught by someone who, in the normal scheme of things, you'd be teaching. Nor was I the most patient instructor. The fact that she'd never driven was one thing, but her ignorance of fundamental principles was so profound it seemed willful. She didn't notice street signs until I pointed them out to her. Worse, she was prone to panic. Once, when we were working on parallel parking, she forgot she was in reverse and accelerated when she felt the car moving backward, thinking that more gas was called for—despite my screaming, "Brake! Brake!"—and remained fully committed to this misconception until we plowed backward through somebody's front yard and totaled a saguaro cactus. The next day I couldn't coax her back behind the wheel without making two promises—that we'd give parallel parking a pass for a day or two and that, no matter what she did, I wouldn't yell at her.

Gradually, we moved from the relative safety of residential neighborhoods out onto busy Indian School Road. As time grew short we embarked on real-life outings with genuine purposes, to the supermarket or the drugstore. She always parked in the most remote reaches of the lot, where she was unlikely to encounter other cars or need to use reverse gear. We made a couple practice runs to her new place of employment, first during off-hours, then under more realistic rush-hour conditions. She got better. Not good—that would never happen—but hardly the menace her son had been a month earlier, towing a trailer down the interstate. At once terrified and game, she gripped the wheel as if expecting a sudden impact at any moment, and I came to realize that fear was probably her best defense against catastrophe. To see my mother grabbing hold like that was to understand that her mind, unlike that of 99 percent of drivers who were far more skilled and experienced, would never wander, even for an instant, from the task at hand.

On the morning of her road test she took an extra half pill with her coffee so her hands wouldn't shake, and by the time we arrived at the Department of Motor Vehicles, she was wearing a smile so serene that I feared her examiner would take in at a glance that she was pharmaceutically impaired, but he didn't. While they were gone I mentally drafted a contingency plan to call the university registrar and say I'd be a week or two late and beg them please, *please,* not to give my dorm room away.

What I dreaded most was having to explain what was happening. No, I couldn't predict exactly when I'd be joining my classmates, as it kind of depended on when my mother passed her driver's test. What if I were asked to assess her chances? Or if the registrar wanted to know how it was that a woman in her forties in this day and age had never driven a car until two weeks ago? Would he have my file on his desk as we spoke? Would he say, *Oh, right—Russo. The one from Gloversville. No wonder.* I was still working on my side of this imaginary conversation when I heard my mother's laughter from all the way across the room. She tossed her head girlishly as she approached, with her examiner, a small man a good fifteen years her junior, as firmly in tow as a dog on a leash. "And this is my son," she was saying, "the one I've been telling you about."

"Your mom did fine," the man said as we shook hands. "She didn't run over a single cactus."

Then he wished her luck on her new job, and they shook hands, and he and I shook hands again, one big happy, complicit family. "What a *nice* man," my mother said when we parted, loud enough for him to hear.

To celebrate, we went to a restaurant for lunch, and my mother ordered a Bloody Mary.

"You actually told him about backing over that saguaro?" I said.

"He thought that was the funniest thing he'd ever heard. They're apparently quite expensive."

I'd suspected as much, which was why, after quickly swapping seats, we'd hightailed it out of there and I'd chosen an entirely new neighborhood to practice in when we resumed parallel parking.

She showed me the temporary license she'd been given. "Hey, you know what this means?" I said. "You're free." Because every fifteen-year-old knows that a driver's license is really about freedom, and I figured my mother, given how desperately she longed for true independence, would register the symbolism. But she just looked at me strangely. After all, she wasn't fifteen; she was forty-five, and failing to learn would've sent her straight back to Helwig Street.

She wasn't blind to the magnitude of the moment, though, and when her drink came she reached across the booth and patted my hand. "Ricko-Mio," she said, her smile less serene now, more loopy, "we did it."

Which was true. There were a few small things left on the to-do list, but nothing important or difficult. "*You* did it," I said. Aware of how much all this had cost her, I was suddenly and unexpectedly proud of her, so proud it didn't seem to matter that what we'd done was in fact borderline moronic. And part of me understood, too, what this unforeseen pride meant—that like my grandfather, I hadn't believed she was capable of much of anything, really. I was proud she'd proved us both wrong, but also surprised. "In fact," I said, "seeing where we were a couple weeks ago, I'm not sure how you managed to pull it off."

"Well," she said, looking so deeply inward now that I knew what she'd say next before she said it. "I just gave myself a good talking-to."

ALL THESE YEARS later it seems incredible to me that after helping me get settled at the university she drove back to Phoenix on her own. Not that it was terribly difficult. We could see the I-10 freeway ramp from the restaurant where we ate that last dinner together. She'd get on the interstate and not get off until she came to the Indian School Road exit, and she'd stay on that until she reached her apartment. It was late August, so it was still light out when she left. It would be dark by the time she got to Phoenix, but the traffic wouldn't be bad. Of course if the Gray Death broke down in the desert she'd be all alone, and even if she could find a pay phone, what possible good would it do to call me? I don't think I worried about any of that. I'd badly underestimated her, as well as our escape vehicle in recent weeks, and they'd both taught me not to. They'd make it fine.

Indeed, as I walked back to campus along busy Speedway Boulevard, I had a profound sense that my mother's life and my own had just diverged, probably for good. I'd be with her for Thanksgiving, and again over the Christmas holidays between semesters. But I'd seen my father before leaving Gloversville, and he'd offered to pay my union dues while I was away at school. That way, if I wanted to come home for the summer, I could get a well-paid construction job, and I'd already decided to do just that. Eighteen was legal drinking age in New York, and he'd begun to show more interest in me since my birthday. By next summer my grandparents would have rented the upstairs flat on Helwig Street, but they had a spare bedroom and would be happy to see me. I could paint the house on weekends to save them some money. I already missed both of them terribly, and for the first time felt the full guilt of having abandoned them. Somehow I'd try to set this right.

My mother didn't factor into any of these plans. Hey, she had the new life she'd wanted for so long. She had people her own age and a nice apartment and parties on weekends and nobody looking over her shoulder, second-guessing her every decision and criticizing her for having a little fun. If the Death didn't die and she got a couple raises, her new ends might just meet. Why shouldn't things work out for her? After all, Phoenix seemed to be the city of fresh starts, of rising from the ashes. There were lots of single men around. And with me finally out of her way, there'd be opportunities for the kind of romance I knew she craved, maybe even marriage, though I doubted she had much interest in that. She just wanted to dress up and go dancing or out to dinner someplace nice now and then. There was no longer any reason she shouldn't have her wish. Back in Gloversville, her mantra had always been that we'd be just fine as long as we had each other, but that pact—unsustainable between a mother who would grow old and a son who'd eventually marry and have children of his own—could now be honorably dissolved by both parties. That's what our long journey across America, all those scary on- and off-ramps, had been about. As she herself had put it, "Ricko-Mio, we did it."

And if we'd done it, it stood to reason that it must be finished, right?

A Diagnosis

*D*ON'T DO IT.

That was my father-in-law's advice in a nutshell. He was not an unkind man, but he'd met my mother at the wedding and, like everyone else, he'd witnessed her fragile condition and sensed how near she was to unraveling. It would also have been clear how dependent she was on me, that if I ever left the room she'd nervously watch the spot I'd disappeared from until I returned. So when his daughter told him that my mother wanted to move in with us until she could find a job and start a new life in Tucson, he warned her that it would be a terrible mistake. "If you let that woman in," he said, "you'll never be rid of her."

She'd telephoned that morning in the throes of a full-blown panic attack. There was a three-hour time difference between New York and Arizona, and she'd waited as long as she could, but it was still early and also a Saturday, so Barbara and I were asleep. I'd been expecting the call for days, actually. My mother and I talked pretty regularly, so I knew where she was in the never-ending cycle of her anxieties. Sometimes venting to me did the trick, releasing some stuck emotional valve, allowing some of the pressure a means of escape, after which she'd pull herself together, give herself a good talking-to, and thereby avert coming completely unglued. "Can't you understand?" she'd sobbed. "Doesn't it matter that I'm a *person*? Don't I have a right to a *life,* like anybody else? How long am I expected to live in a *cage*?"

The cage was once again 36 Helwig Street, where she'd been living for a couple years. Phoenix had gone well for a time, but ultimately badly. She'd fallen in love with a man who looked like Sam Shepard and was about as laconic. He wore jeans and cowboy boots and drove a pickup truck. Then suddenly he was gone, and she was devastated. The story she told me was that they'd gotten too serious, too quickly. He had no desire to get married, so he'd left the state in hopes of forgetting her. That last part didn't sound like the man in question, and a friend of hers later confided that he hadn't left Arizona, or even Phoenix, or, for that matter, the neighborhood. He'd bolted once he discovered how intense my mother was about *him,* moving to another apartment house a few blocks away, where he was now seeing someone else. When my mother spotted his truck in the lot, it sent her into a tailspin. Had she mentioned, her friend wondered, that she'd lost her job at U-Haul? Well, no, she hadn't, but she did the next time we spoke, saying that it was okay, that she'd hated the job from the start. The company wasn't well run, nothing like the old GE in Schenectady, which for her always represented the gold standard of employment. What had she been thinking to leave it? she wondered out loud. Just imagine if she'd stayed. How many promotions would she have fielded by now? Just imagine her salary.

It didn't take her long to find another job, though it was no better, and she had no safety net if something went wrong, which was making her nervous. Her doctor had agreed to up the dosage on her Valium, but she didn't like the way it made her feel. While she wanted to stop taking the pills entirely, she needed them to stay functional. Something was amiss at the apartment house, too. It had been so fun-loving and gay at the beginning, but the parties had turned dark, and there were drugs now. (By then it was the mid-Seventies, so maybe.) Worst of all was the driving—the traffic, the heat, the lack of air-conditioning. Something was going to have to change, or she'd suffer a nervous breakdown.

Then, to my surprise, on the heels of the fleeing cowboy, there was suddenly another man in her life. Several years younger and recently divorced, he was clearly crazy about her. I'd met the man and liked him, though something didn't seem right. She was always a sucker for style, and the men she was usually drawn to—like my father and the most recent fugitive—were invariably handsome and had a certain swagger, a boyish, self-destructive charm, a hint of danger. Russ had exactly none of that going for him, but he was good-natured and solid, the kind of man who might actually be good for my mother if she could learn to see past his unromantic virtues.

"Well, I think he loves you," I said when she asked my opinion about what she should do. "Do you love him?"

She didn't answer, so I said, "It sounds like you have a decision to make," and she agreed that she did. Neither of us needed to articulate the exact nature of the dilemma: she could marry a man she didn't love or return to Gloversville.

The marriage lasted a couple years, one in Phoenix and another in San Francisco, then crashed and burned. After the split she moved to nearby Pacifica, which sat under a permanent bank of dense, wet fog. Her apartment was situated on a cliff, and from it you could hear the waves pounding on the beach below, and there she went about the business of once again putting herself back together. She had no job, though, and no means of getting one. I'd inherited the Gray Death when she and Russ went to San Francisco and was willing to give it back, but she said no, she was through with driving.

So, when the money from the small divorce settlement ran out, there was nothing to do but return to upstate New York. It was midsemester, and I was now in grad school, but I stole a few days and flew to San Francisco, where I rented a truck, packed her books and other possessions, put them in storage, and promised to drive them to Gloversville that summer. My grandparents found money for a one-way plane ticket to Albany. My aunt and uncle picked her up and drove her to Helwig Street, where my grandparents had evicted their upstairs tenant to make room for her. She arrived in Gloversville with two suitcases and an official narrative. She had *not* failed to make a new life for herself out west. Moving to Arizona had *not* been a mistake. She was *not* returning home in defeat, but rather because her father was failing fast, on oxygen all the time and for the most part confined to his armchair. The burden of his declining health on her mother was too much, so she was returning to help out. As with so many of my mother's narratives, this one was designed for people who knew better—her parents, her sister and brother-in-law, me. She never cared whether people believed her, simply that her version of events was never publicly questioned.

Being back in Gloversville worked for a while. She found a job and bought some furniture on credit. My grandfather's condition was truly grave, and for a while her own problems paled by comparison. My mother had always adored him, and the rift caused by our departure for Arizona got mended. Further disputes were now out of the question; he had all he could do just to draw his next breath. For over a year she and my grandmother lived to the rhythm of his gasps until finally they stopped. Then they were alone in the Helwig Street house, two women who'd never seen eye to eye about anything. While my grandfather lived, they'd managed to coexist; neither had wanted to upset him, but with him gone the conflict resumed. To the old resentments—my grandmother questioning my mother's decisions and offering unsolicited advice—was added another, far more toxic dispute. They simply could not agree on who my grandfather had been. To my grandmother, he was a loving husband, a model of responsibility and duty, the kind of man who quietly endured what could not be cured; to my mother he'd been a rebel, trapped just as she was in a town he hated, in roles as husband and father he'd never wanted but from which he could never escape. On top of all this, a recession hit, and my mother was laid off, and there wasn't much to do with the day's long hours except to take stock: once again stuck in Gloversville with no friends, no money, no future, no life. All of which had led to that Saturday morning when she'd called to ask me how long any human being was expected to live in a cage. There was only one person in the whole world who really cared about her, who understood and could help her, and that was me. She needed to make a new beginning, but she could hardly do it by herself, with no one to call her own.

At the time my wife and I were living in a fourteen-foot-wide mobile home that we'd parked in a remote trailer park on the outskirts of Tucson, where rental spaces were cheapest. It had two bedrooms, one on each end, the architectural wisdom of which we didn't fully appreciate until my mother came to live with us. It cost twelve grand, probably more than my grandfather had paid for the house on Helwig Street, and to me a terrifying sum to owe. How could we ever pay back that kind of money? My grad school stipend paid less than two grand for teaching two sections of freshman composition per semester. Barbara was a secretary at a tiny, fast-failing electronics firm that her father had started up with another engineer from Hughes Aircraft. They'd called the company Iota, which by the time we got married seemed to summarize its chances of surviving another year. For those reasons I'd hoped, right up until we closed, that the finance company would take a good look at us, come to its senses, and refuse us the loan.

"She'd only be with us until she finds a job and can afford her own apartment," I assured my wife. "She doesn't want to live with us."

"There's a recession here, too," Barbara pointed out. "What will she do in this trailer all day when we're gone? How will she get to job interviews? If she gets a job, how will she get back and forth to work? Who's going to hire someone who can't hold her hands still?"

All good questions. With no answers anybody would want to offer.

I didn't even recognize her getting off the plane. Too poor to travel, we hadn't actually seen each other in the year and a half since the wedding, by far the longest we'd ever been apart. She had to say my name, and I had to connect the sound of her voice to the frail, elderly woman coming toward me. Her hair had gone mostly gray, but it wasn't that. She seemed about half the size of the woman who a few short years before had climbed behind the wheel of a car she only half knew how to drive and pointed it toward Phoenix and the new life she was betting everything on. Had she been like this at the wedding? Caught up in the event and my own happiness, had I failed to notice? When had she become so *tiny*? Or was it me, simply that I was looking at her with new eyes? After all, I was now married. At least symbolically my mother's place in my life had been diminished. But, no, it was more than that. The way she came toward me had less to do with how I saw her than how she saw herself. In her *own* eyes she was about half her former size. When I held out my arms, she stumbled, nearly falling into my embrace. "Ricko-Mio," she said. "Always there. Always my rock."

SHE WAS IN terrible shape, shattered and barely functional. Determined to get back on her feet as soon as possible, my mother immediately scoured the help-wanted ads but on most days didn't make a single call, unable to control her voice, barely able to hold on to the phone because her hands shook so badly. On better days she'd set up interviews around my teaching responsibilities, then cancel them as the time approached and she became too nervous. I'd seen her in bad shape before, but this was new. It was as if her world had gotten smaller, or the part of it she felt safe in had. For Barbara and me the trailer was suddenly too small, its common areas, especially the kitchen, too cramped. We were constantly in one another's way. That was what my mother seemed to like best about it. Back in Gloversville, after my grandfather's death, she'd been living by herself in our old flat with the few pieces of furniture she'd bought and could no longer make the payments on. Whole days had gone by, she told me, when she never heard the sound of another human voice. The fact that we were so crowded in our trailer was having a healing effect. She was no longer alone.

It also seemed to help that I was never gone for more than

a few hours. Barbara had a nine-to-five job and left for work early, but my mother and I began each day over coffee, mapping out what she'd try to get done in our absence, and in the evening we all ate dinner together. I gave her my teaching schedule, so she knew when my classes got out and roughly when to expect me back. I knew to call if something unexpected came up at the university, because each afternoon she positioned herself at the window and waited for the Gray Death (yes, still alive) to pull up beside the trailer. Normally I'd have graded my papers and prepared for classes on campus, but things ran more smoothly if I didn't leave her alone too long. Gradually, her condition did improve. She was able to cut back on the number of pills she was taking, and the tremor in her hands became less pronounced. She set up more interviews and actually made it to a couple of them.

The problem was that though my mother was doing better, my wife and I were doing worse. She was finding reasons to stay later at work, and I couldn't blame her. Each night there were three of us at the dinner table, but mostly my mother talked to me as if Barbara weren't there. It was almost as if she'd forgotten I was married, that this extra, unnecessary person was my wife and not some girlfriend I'd soon tire of, or vice versa. She certainly didn't dislike or resent Barbara and often remembered to thank her for opening up her home. It was my wife's *existence* she couldn't quite account for, as if she were a hologram, and when I asked Barbara a direct question, my mother often answered it. At the end of the evening, after we'd done the dishes, Barbara and I retreated to our bedroom as early as we decently could, and after turning out the lights we crawled into bed and whispered all the things we normally would've talked about over dinner. I think we both imagined my mother on the other side of the door, desperate to give us her input. We could no longer have friends over and felt guilty (or at least I did) if we went out someplace and didn't include her.

Not that we'd have gone out much. Iota Engineering was then in its death throes, sometimes unable to make its payroll. One month Barbara was paid in office furniture, and she had little choice but to start looking for another job. It was against this stark financial backdrop that we began to make weekend trips to places like FedMart to start furnishing the kitchen of the apartment my mother didn't yet have. It seemed like a smart idea to do it little by little. A new frying pan or a set of cheap cutlery cheered my mother by bringing into imaginative focus the day when she'd be officially back on her feet and living, as she liked to put it, independently. It wasn't just for her that we did this, of course. Buying the pan also allowed Barbara and me to believe that day was coming. One Saturday, though, I went too far and put too many things into the shopping cart, as if to hasten its arrival, and when I looked up Barbara was gone. I found her in the car, in tears. I'd spent money we simply didn't have. Nor could we borrow it. Her father hadn't drawn a salary in months, so her parents' situation, with most of her nine brothers and sisters still living at home, was as dire as ours. There was simply no one in either of our families who had two nickels to rub together. And of course I made the mistake of saying we'd been fools to ever buy the trailer, and the look on my wife's face conveyed clearly what she was too kind to say. We'd been fools, all right, but not about the trailer. Even if we assumed the day would finally come when my mother had recovered sufficiently to live on her own, what would be left of us?

But eventually, that day did come, along with a great many others, and somehow there was still an "us" for my wife and me to protect and cherish. Indeed, over time our trials would appear to illustrate the old saw that what doesn't kill you makes you stronger. The threads we were dangling by in Tucson, both financial and emotional, proved more sinewy than we'd imagined. They would need to be.

THE FURNISHED APARTMENT my mother finally rented in Tucson reminded her of the one she'd loved in Phoenix, and she found a job she could get to by bus. Weekends I took her to the grocery store and wherever else she needed to go. Otherwise, Barbara and I returned as best we could to the routines of our young married life and told ourselves that maybe it would all work out. But then summer was upon us with its pulverizing heat. My mother's apartment was several blocks from the bus stop, and the buses weren't necessarily air-conditioned, so she often arrived at work already wilted, with eight hours still to go. She ate lunch at her desk, there being no restaurants within walking distance, at least in the midday heat, and there were no sidewalks anyway. In July came the monsoon rains, the skies darkening ominously every afternoon right as she got off work, and the downpours, though brief, were apocalyptic. She must've felt like the physical world was mocking her, because by the time she got home, drenched to her skin, the skies would be blue again and steam rising from the asphalt, the air not just hot but humid. "What an awful, awful place," she lamented, exactly what she'd said that morning in Phoenix after learning she wouldn't be working for GE anymore.

Ironically, what ended up doing her in was neither Tucson, with its heat and monsoons, nor the job she hated (her new company poorly run, nothing like GE), nor the fact that she'd made no friends, but rather the return of her emotional equilibrium. One of the ironies of my mother's condition was that her periodic tranquillity was usually a mixed blessing. Panic might cause her to spin out of control, but once she got her bearings again, she could see beyond her own torment. Back in Gloversville, her desperation to make one last grab at a fulfilling life hadn't allowed her to imagine what that would be like in Tucson. It *had* to be better because it couldn't be any worse. In her mind's eye everything she saw was on a Gloversville scale, only better. She pictured me living nearby, down the street, maybe, or right around the corner. But Tucson was like Phoenix, a sprawling city of identically ugly intersections, where you were always half an hour away from anywhere else. It was a sea of cars, and she didn't have or want one. Being "close" in Tucson wasn't ten minutes by foot; it was twenty minutes by car—and much longer if you were living, say, in a remote trailer park.

Worse, her failure to accurately predict her own life in Tucson was compounded by her inability to understand *ours*. She had no idea how hard we were working, me on my Ph.D., Barbara on supporting us while I did. Even before my mother's arrival, we'd been stretched thin in virtually every respect. As short as we were on money, we had even less time. I needed my Sundays for grading papers, and on Friday and Saturday nights, for extra cash, I was a singer in a popular restaurant. Barbara's large family all lived in Tucson, which provided plenty of other obligations. But whenever something unexpectedly came up in my mother's life, I always did my best to accommodate her, and she could tell it wasn't easy. "You're always there when I need you," she'd said one day, gratefully patting my hand in the dentist's office after she'd chipped a tooth. The plan we'd developed back at the trailer was intended to restore her independence, and its major components were now in place. She had an apartment and a job. What was dawning on her, though, was that none of this was sustainable. The truth was that she needed me, at least emotionally, all the time. The only thing that could work in the long run would be a version of the old Helwig Street model in which each of us was central to the other's daily existence. But eventually, Barbara and I would have children, and as a father I'd have even less time to devote to her. And when I finished the Ph.D., my university career would begin, and who knew where that would take me? Back in Gloversville it might have seemed that we were separated only by geography, by all those miles, but now she understood that our separation was not only more profound than she'd imagined but was in fact only going to get worse.

By the time the holidays rolled around, she'd given herself a good talking-to. Coming to Tucson had been a mistake. It was time to admit that. And also, starting over in her midfifties was, well, too late. She hated Gloversville, God knew, but maybe it was the right place for her, maybe the only place. Her mother had welcomed her back before and would again. They would simply have to find a way to get along. Toward that end, she had a new, better idea. Instead of living upstairs in our old flat, she'd move into the spare bedroom downstairs, and they would share expenses. The upstairs flat could be rented, further bolstering their bottom line, taking financial stress completely out of the equation. And, to put my worries to rest, she pointed out that it wasn't like we'd never see each other again. There were far more colleges and universities east of the Mississippi than west of it, so I'd more likely end up teaching somewhere back east, and we could spend our holidays together. She'd worked it all out, just as she had that long-ago plan to come west with me in the first place, letting me in on the details only after her own mind was made up. I wasn't asked what I thought of the decision, simply informed of it, which was just as well.

Maybe coming to Tucson had been a bad decision, as she said, but returning to Gloversville would be another. What I couldn't give voice to was my growing certainty that my mother was lost in some labyrinth of her own thoughts and impulses, and that if she was ever going to escape the maze, she'd have done so already. Since leaving Gloversville myself, I'd come to understand that this had also been my grandfather's fear. I remembered that last day on Helwig Street when he'd watched from the front window, gulping air from his oxygen tank, as my friends and I loaded the U-Haul. Over the long months of bitter conflict, his anxiety had morphed into resignation in the face of his daughter's tidal determination, but when my eyes met his I didn't yet understand the true nature of his concern. He was worried about what would become of my mother, of course, but also what would become of me. Even if he'd had the desire, he lacked the breath to say all this, and anyway it would have been a terrible betrayal of the daughter he couldn't stop loving, regardless. Probably less harmful, he must have reasoned, to maintain the long-established family narrative. My mother suffered from nerves. So did lots of people.

Ironically, the one person who ever openly questioned that narrative was my father. He wasn't one to indulge regret or apologize, but the summer I turned twenty-one we were working road construction together in Albany, and he must've decided the time was right to explain his absence during my childhood. We'd stopped at half-a-dozen roadhouses on the way home, as was our dangerous habit, and were very drunk. "I should've thought about you more," he admitted, "but you were easy to forget. There was always something going on, a horse at the track that couldn't lose or some poker game. You seemed to be doing fine without me." When he paused, I figured he'd said his piece, but then he added one last thing. "And anyway, I couldn't be your father without being married to that crazy woman." The expression on my face then must have been strange, because he leaned back on his bar stool so he could really take me in. "You *do* know your mother's nuts, right?"

I don't know what I looked like, of course, but I recall being for a time unable to speak. I probably just sat there with my mouth open, a series of unwelcome emotions washing over me in waves. First anger at the seeming ease with which my father, who had no right to do so, had offered his judgment. After all, if my mother was crazy, at the very least he was a contributing factor. But even more powerful than anger was a totally unexpected surge of relief, because his verdict was no sooner rendered than I realized it was true, that I'd known this myself at least since the morning in Phoenix when she'd finally come clean about not really having a job at GE awaiting her there; and probably, truth be told, some part of me had known it for much longer. How many meltdowns, followed by good talking-tos, had I witnessed as a boy, too frightened to draw the necessary inference? Later on, as an adolescent, how many times had I suppressed the terrible possibility that something in my mother was off-kilter? Hadn't I also suspected all along that other family members—my grandparents and aunt at a minimum—also knew this but refused to say anything? Now, for the first time, I understood how lonely I'd been in my fears and suspicions, how alone I'd felt in the possession of adult knowledge to which I was hardly entitled.

And, finally, I felt guilty. That I'd come to the same heartless conclusion as my father was a terrible betrayal, surely. I don't recall whether that came right away or later. I only know there's been enough to last a lifetime. How else to explain my willingness to jeopardize my young marriage a decade later and, as the next three decades unspooled and my mother's condition worsened, the many times I'd repeat that same mistake, refusing to acknowledge the primacy of other loyalties subsequent to those forged on Helwig Street. Suffice to say that my mother wasn't the only one caught in a dangerous loop of repetitive behavior.

NOT LONG AFTER she returned to Gloversville from Tucson, I began a decade-long academic nomadship during which I jumped from job to job, trying to teach and be a writer at the same time. For a while, after our daughters came along, we were even poorer than we'd been as graduate students. And I was a bad boy. Caring not a whit about tenure and promotion, I thumbed my nose at the advice of department chairs about what I needed to do to succeed in the university. I left jobs for other jobs that paid less but offered more time out of the classroom. In the summer, when many of my colleagues taught extra classes, I wrote stories and spent money we didn't have on postage to submit them to magazines. I wrote manically, obsessively, but also, for a time, not very well. I wrote about crime and cities and women and other things I knew very little about in a language very different from my own natural voice, which explained why the editors weren't much interested.

My first full-time job was as an assistant professor at a branch campus of Penn State University. Altoona was a good day's drive from Gloversville, close enough for holiday visits but too far for my mother to expect much more. We continued to talk on the phone at least once a week, and these calls were for her a lifeline. I knew things weren't going well. She'd moved into the spare bedroom downstairs as planned, but she and my grandmother, who was by then in her eighties and crippled by arthritis, still weren't getting along. They liked different TV shows and different food, and rather than come to an accommodation my mother insisted on cordoning off their existences. Since the dining and living rooms were roughly the same size, they set up their own camps. They had no choice but to share the kitchen, though my mother refused to cook or to allow my grandmother to, arguing she was the one who'd have to clean up. So at lunchtime each made her own sandwich using her own personal ingredients, and for dinner each warmed her own frozen dinner in the oven. Afterward, they watched their favorite shows on their competing televisions, bickering endlessly about whose volume was turned up too high. My grandmother seemed to understand that this was lunatic behavior, but confronting her daughter would only have made matters worse. With her husband gone, the balance of power had shifted. Short of threatening to toss her out, something my grandmother never would've done, she had little leverage, so gradually my mother's will became law. When we visited, usually during the holidays, they strove for a truce, but you could tell they were unused to speaking to each other beyond demanding that the rival television be turned down. One day my father stopped by to say hello, took in the arrangement at a glance—my grandmother's furniture crammed into one room, my mother's into the other, the two TVs a few feet apart blaring different shows—and regarded my mother for a long moment, then said, "Jean. What the hell's *wrong* with you?"

Not long afterward he was diagnosed with lung cancer, and this more or less coincided with my taking a new job in New Haven, which meant I'd be only four hours from Gloversville instead of eight; given the deteriorating situation there, closer seemed to me, if not better, at least more advantageous. My father did his chemotherapy and radiation, and his cancer went into remission before it ultimately returned even more aggressively. Finally, too sick to care for himself, he was admitted into the VA hospital in Albany, where I visited him every other weekend. He seemed less concerned about his own mortality than not having anybody to bet his daily doubles at the OTB. "You going over to Helwig Street when you leave here?" he'd ask, incredulous, like a man who'd dodged a bullet even more dangerous than death. "*That's* some crazy shit going on over there."

In the spring of our second year in New Haven I sold my first novel, as a result of which I was offered my first real job as a writer. Until then I'd been a teacher with a writing habit that was tolerated but not necessarily encouraged. The new job, in Carbondale, Illinois, offered everything I'd wanted for the last decade—a real writing program, good colleagues, time to do my own work. But it was too far away, I knew. Instead of being four hours from Gloversville, I'd now be three days. My mother needed me closer, not farther away. I explained why I had to take the job, and she agreed I'd be a fool not to, but not long after we were settled in Carbondale, I got what would be the last of those frantic Helwig Street phone calls from my mother demanding to know why she didn't deserve a life the same as anybody else and how long she was expected to remain locked in a cage. I called my aunt to see if things were as bad as they seemed and learned they were actually worse, much worse. There was a lot going on, most of it old: conflicts not only unresolved but also unresolvable. But one new thing my aunt mentioned scared me. My grandmother had been prescribed a new medication in capsule form, to be taken with food, and my mother had somehow gotten it into her head that this meant the capsules needed to be ground up in her food, which she then proceeded to do over my grandmother's tearful objections. When my aunt discovered what was going on and confronted her sister, explaining that the medication simply should be taken *with* meals, she became unhinged, screaming that if anything happened to their mother, it would be my aunt's fault. She had shouldered the entire burden of my grandmother's deteriorating health for years, she claimed, expected to make every single decision, but if her judgment was going to be questioned, now or ever, then she wanted nothing more to do with it. My aunt could take over all those duties and see how well she liked them. Apparently this fracas had precipitated the call to Carbondale. My aunt knew and was very fond of my wife, and knew we had our hands full with new jobs and two small daughters, but I could tell she was also worried sick for my grandmother, and when I asked if I should come get my mother, she reluctantly agreed it might be for the best.

By the time I got to Gloversville, she'd calmed down some. The knowledge that I was coming, that I'd be there by week's end, allowed her to step back from the precipice, but she was clearly in terrible shape, far worse than when she'd come to live with us in Tucson. At the time I owned a pickup truck into which we loaded her things, mostly books. What didn't fit was left behind. I'd borrowed a camper shell so we could lock everything up at night when we checked into motels. Together, we drove back across the country on the same route we'd taken twenty years before. The truck had air-conditioning, but my mother suffered one panic attack after another, and she swore she couldn't breathe, so we had to drive with the windows open to the August heat. Between these fits she regaled me with stories about how awful the last few years had been, detailing every single responsibility that was hers and hers alone, how abusive her sister and mother had been. "You have no idea how cruel they were," she said, over and over. "I kept it all a secret."

As we made our slow journey west, my wife was busy trying to find a place for her to live. Before I headed to Gloversville, we'd negotiated as best we could the terms for how all this would go. Assuming she wasn't a danger, my mother would stay with us until September. She was retired now, on Social Security, so she didn't need to work, and she qualified for elderly housing, if we could find it. Halfway to Illinois I called Barbara, who said there was an opening at the senior-citizen tower, exactly the sort of place I knew my mother would veto.

The next day I explained patiently that the apartment would only be temporary until we could find something better, that it was five minutes from our house, and she'd have the rest of August with us to get back on her feet and orient herself to her new environment before moving in. Since her only other option was returning to Gloversville, she had to go along with this, though she had a stipulation. The tower had to be only for the elderly, with no Section 8 residents. She refused to live with crazy people.

She also wanted to know if my driver's-side window was rolled down all the way, because she couldn't breathe. I knew how she felt. I couldn't either.

FIVE YEARS LATER, in 1991, I was offered a teaching position at Colby College in Maine. What made the position especially attractive was that it was part-time, a relative rarity in academia. At long last I was earning some money from my writing, almost enough—maybe, if nothing went wrong—to live on. At Colby I'd have more time to write and health insurance despite my part-time status, as well as a tuition subsidy for our daughters. If things went well, I could imagine writing full-time in a few years. We were also anxious to put southern Illinois's buggy, humid, tornado-ripe summers behind us, not to mention its passive-aggressive religious fundamentalists. I was tired of answering the door on Sunday morning to find strangers wanting to talk about Jesus. When we politely (for the most part) declined, they'd peer inside and see all the books, then shake their heads and advise us to put away our pride. "All them books don't amount to nothin'," they'd tell me, "not if you don't know the *Good* Book."

There were, however, compelling reasons to stay put. Barbara liked her job, and our daughters had their friends, and I was pretty sure the university would match whatever Colby offered. And of course there was my mother. She'd changed apartments twice since I brought her to Carbondale, and while she hated it there, she at least was settled. Like she always did after leaving Gloversville, she now remembered it fondly as the home from which she'd been exiled. She called every week to talk to her sister and mother and ended all these conversations by saying how much she loved and missed them, how lucky they were not to live in the Midwest. During the long spring and summer months, when the tornado watches beeped and inched incessantly along the bottom of television screens, she phoned with a familiar lament: "What an awful, awful place."

She was anxious to go to Maine, of course, because she'd be closer to home, but could she make the trip? It would be, no matter how we handled it, a logistical nightmare. Say we went to Maine, found a place, moved in, and then returned for my mother. Well, she couldn't be left alone for longer than it took milk to spoil because it would, literally, spoil. Even more important, her emotional well-being was tied to our proximity. On any occasion when we'd be gone for just a week—taking the girls to Disney World, for example—it was necessary to let her know well in advance so she could accustom herself to the idea, and then she required telephone numbers not only for every place we'd be staying but also for various friends in case she needed backup. Still her anxiety level always rose to fever pitch in the days before we left, and afterward we were pretty sure she upped the dosage of her meds on her own authority. Since it might take us a month to get settled in Maine, leaving her behind was simply out of the question. The opposite scenario—setting her up in an apartment in a strange new place, then returning to Illinois to go through our own move—would be, if anything, worse. Therefore, we'd have to make the move together, putting everything in storage until we found accommodations.

Actually, after I accepted Colby's offer, we discovered all this was going to be even more difficult. What few decent apartments were available in the Waterville area got snapped up seasonally by faculty and staff, so finding a place for my mother was going to be a challenge. On top of that, the housing market there was tight and expensive. Barbara made two exploratory trips that spring, saw numerous listings, and came back dejected both times. There was nothing even remotely as nice as the house we were selling in Carbondale. Worse, it *wasn't* selling. After two months, no one had even insulted us with a lowball offer, whereas in Waterville, where we wanted to live because of the schools, anything good got snapped up before we could see it. Since we'd be moving over the summer, we were advised to rent a camp on one of the nearby lakes and look at our leisure. If we saw something we liked we could make an offer within twenty-four hours.

As our departure date approached, my mother again

showed signs of coming unglued. There was just so much to be done, she kept saying, and she had to do it all herself. Actually, I kept reminding her, there was nothing for her to do. I'd hired a mover, scheduling her things to be loaded onto the truck the day before the same mover added our own. I would pack up her books and anything that wasn't going on the truck myself. The night before the move, she'd stay with us. Yes, she said, but that still left hundreds of other tasks she'd have to do, though when I asked what they were, she'd collapse into the nearest armchair and claim she was too exhausted to think. Nor could we agree on how to handle the simplest details. It was June, and the temperatures already in triple digits, but she was adamant that we drive to the phone company to terminate her service, then to the cable company, and so forth. We could do that by phone, I pointed out. No, she said, she'd never had much *luck* with the phone. She was afraid the utility companies wouldn't refund her deposits, and that was money she couldn't afford to lose. I promised to make good on any losses, but she didn't want my money; she wanted *her* money. The day her stuff was to be loaded on the truck, it was more than a hundred degrees by nine in the morning, and when the truck pulled up and two skinny black kids got out, I knew we were in trouble. The driver couldn't have been more than eighteen, and the other looked about fifteen and weighed a hundred and ten pounds tops. "Stay here," I told her, then went outside to talk to the driver and sign the paperwork. "My mother's in a bit of a state," I warned him. "I'll try to keep her out of your way." I'd hoped to convey this vital information to the other kid, too, but he'd gone directly inside. He was in there for about ten seconds when I heard my mother wail, "Oooh! Oooh! *Oooh!*" as if he were jabbing her with a hat pin. Arriving on the scene, I saw that he'd picked up my mother's credenza by one end and was intent on taking it outside. It wasn't a heavy piece of furniture. He'd taken one look at it, sussed out that it was made of pressed sawdust, not wood, and hoisted it into the air. "You'll break it!" my mother was screaming at him, her hands over her mouth. "You'll *break* it!"

In the car, she sat there, her face in her hands, still picturing the kid with the credenza. "You need to calm down," I told her. "If it gets broken, I'll replace it."

"But I *love* it," she said.

"Mom," I said. "It's from Kmart."

It took a good minute for her to respond to this unwelcome fact. "Don't you have things that *you* love?" I didn't answer, and she was quiet until we pulled into the driveway of the house we'd be leaving the next morning. "Do you really think I'm not trying?" she said, her hands shaking and bottom lip quivering. "Because I am. I hope you never know how hard."

There wasn't much to say to that. She was trying. As hard as she could. As was often the case with my mother, it was her utter lack of success that strained credulity.

AND SO WHATEVER didn't fit into our two small cars went into storage, to be delivered we knew not when to we knew not where. For my mother, who always preferred to settle things wrongly than to leave them unsettled, a nightmare. For all concerned, the next five days turned out to be another. Barbara drove one car, with Emily and Kate listening to music on their headphones in the backseat, my mother riding with me in the other. Officially unraveled now, she suffered one anxiety attack after another, unable to breathe unless all the windows were down, muttering all the while, "Dear God, how much longer?" Our progress was slow, torturous. In the morning it took her a good hour and a half to get ready, and by late afternoon she'd had all she could endure, and we'd have to pull off. She needed a hotel room to herself, which was fine, because by then so did we. She needed another hour or more to shower and dress for dinner, and then we had to scout out the possibilities. "I'm sorry, but really I can't bear it," she'd say if the place was too loud or she could smell grease when we walked in. When we finally found a restaurant she *could* bear, the first thing she did was ask our waiter to turn down the air-conditioning because it was freezing, and often there was something wrong with the table we'd been seated at. What she was hoping for, of course, was never on the menu. "If only they just had a grilled cheese sandwich," she'd lament. "Could you ask if they'd make me one?" My mother never ordered for herself in restaurants. She explained what she wanted and expected me, as the man at the table, to communicate her desires. If a waiter addressed her directly, she'd say, "My son will order for me." Sometimes, depending on just how disappointed she was with the overall proceedings, she'd add, audibly, "If they were professionals, they'd know it's the man who orders." Emily, ever the peacemaker where her grandmother was concerned, would try to appease her. "I don't think that's the way things work anymore, Grandma," she'd say. "Certainly not in T.G.I. Friday's," her sister would add. Most days, I'd about had it by that time. "There are two hundred people in here, Mom. You have to order from the menu." Sometimes Barbara would note that there actually *was* a grilled cheese sandwich on the kiddie menu, which it would then fall to me to order. "That was perfect," my mother would say when she was finished, now in a better mood. "It was all I wanted." By then I'd usually had a couple bottles of beer or a margarita. *Would you please, for the love of God, just shut the fuck up and eat your Jell-O?* That was what I'd have liked to say. Items on the children's menu always came with Jell-O.

Our second day on the road, around dawn, we were awakened by a call from the motel's front desk. During the night somebody had broken into my car, smashing in the windshield with a tire iron. Nothing was stolen, but we couldn't get back on the road until we spent the morning getting the windshield replaced. The front seat and floor were vacuumed, but tiny glass shards had worked their way into the fabric of the seat cushions, and by the time I drove back to the motel where my family anxiously awaited, my undershorts were pink. My mother would now have to ride in the other vehicle. "Which car do you want to drive?" I asked Barbara. That is, would you rather have my mother in your car for the next seven hours or bleed from the ass in mine? After twenty-five years, she was used to such choices. Still, she seemed to debate this one for a long time.

We took a bath towel from the motel and put it down on the seat, and then I slid in gingerly behind the wheel. "Try not to squirm," my wife advised.

I gave her what I hoped was my most appreciative smile. "You too."

WE'D RENTED A large camp on Great Pond for this summer of house and apartment hunting, and the girls immediately claimed its loft for their own. They could listen to music on their headphones without disturbing the adults, and with the lake only a few feet from the back deck, they could swim whenever they wanted, which was always. Late afternoons Kate and I fished, though we never caught anything, and weather permitting I cooked outdoors on the grill. The nights were so perfectly black and quiet we could hear the water lapping gently against the dock, and we fell asleep more often than not to the singing of loons.

Barbara and I divided our two major tasks. Working with a local realtor, she scoured the market. Most of the nicer houses, at least the ones we could afford, were in developments outside town, whereas we wanted to be *in* town, near the college if possible, in the Waterville school district, but the few decent neighborhoods seemed to be out of our price range. One of the good things about moving to a grungy mill town, we'd thought, was that we'd be able to afford a nice house. Apparently we'd thought wrong. Every time Barbara returned from one of these expeditions she seemed more dispirited.

She had company. My job—finding a place for my mother—wasn't any easier. She was better now that we'd gotten off the road but was still a bundle of nerves, and I knew she wasn't going to calm down until things were, as she put it, "settled." That is, until she had an apartment and her belongings were installed and she could get back into her routines. A nice, cozy little one bedroom, bright and airy, carpeted, nothing extravagant. It was fine if this was in an apartment complex, but it had to be for elderly residents only (no families with children). She wanted nothing to do with "assisted living." Because she refused to take money from us—or at least no more than necessary, as on Helwig Street—we quickly determined that she couldn't afford market prices. That meant something subsidized, where her rent would be keyed to her monthly Social Security stipend. Unfortunately, these federal and state subsidies were tied to onerous regulations, the most objectionable of which was that Section 8 "crazies" could not be turned away, and she refused to live with people like that. In theory she didn't object to renting a flat in a private home, but she couldn't abide old plumbing, so the kitchen and bathroom would have to be modern. Unable to climb steep stairs anymore, she would need to be on the first floor, a preference shared by those who owned most of these homes. But finding a downstairs flat was no guarantee, because she hated to hear people walking overhead, so the upstairs floors had to be carpeted. After a week of poring over the ads in the local paper, of pulling up in front of apartments only to drive away immediately if a car was up on blocks at the curb (a Maine specialty) or the yard was infested with weeds or the house itself looked ramshackle, we quickly discovered that the place my mother was looking for simply didn't exist, at least not in Waterville. Once we knew where the clean neighborhoods were, we drove them street by street, hoping a FOR RENT sign might've magically appeared in a window since yesterday, but none ever did, and with each passing day my mother became more and more deflated. Eventually I decided to visit Colby College, ostensibly to introduce myself to my new colleagues, but also hoping to tap some local insider knowledge. Everyone agreed that we'd have to expand our search. The few good apartments in town were quickly rented by college faculty and staff. The time to look was late May, at the end of the school year, not mid-July. Under the circumstances our best bet would be to consider nearby Winslow or Oakland. Several people recommended we try Farmingdale.

Farmingdale, however, was a good half hour away, and given my mother's increasingly fragile condition, that would be stretching it. The apartment she'd envisioned wasn't just bright and clean and airy and carpeted and on the first floor, with updated plumbing, it was right around the corner from our house, the one we hadn't found yet and probably couldn't afford when we did. Even if we could find the perfect house, it wouldn't be perfect if it was so distant. That evening one of my new colleagues called to say that she remembered an apartment complex in Farmingdale on a hill overlooking the Kennebec River, so over dinner, I suggested we drive out there the next day, when it was supposed to be warm and sunny. We could have lunch on the river, then take a peek at the complex. What harm could it do? I didn't expect this weak pitch to succeed, but it did.

The apartments did indeed sit on a hill overlooking the river. They were tidy and clean, the grounds well kept. Better yet, to judge by the sign, an apartment was actually available. "It's an awfully long way from you," my mother said as we pulled into the lot. "It's a good distance from Waterville," I agreed. "The problem is we don't yet know where we're going to end up." Which was true. Just as she and I were expanding our apartment search, so was Barbara expanding hers. One of the nicer houses we'd seen was in Winthrop, a suburb of Augusta, about ten minutes from where we now sat.

In fact the vacancy, a one bedroom on the ground floor, was carpeted, if not as bright or airy as one might have hoped. But the complex looked to be about a decade old, so the plumbing was modern, and I pointed out the cable TV hookup. It was by far the best apartment we'd seen, and I could tell my mother was balancing this with the fact that it wasn't exactly what she'd pictured. She wasn't asking for a lot. Couldn't she, just this once, have what she wanted? In the kitchen, with the apartment manager looking on, she paused to draw her index finger along the surface of the stove.

Outside, noticing another complex farther up the hill, my mother asked about it, because it looked nice.

"That's for families," the woman said. "You said you didn't want that, right?"

"It's awfully close," my mother said. "Do the children come down here?"

"Never," the woman assured her. "The two complexes are completely separate."

"I think we'll keep looking," my mother told her, nodding at me. "My son and his family are going to be in Waterville, and he wouldn't want me to be that far away."

Back in the car, she took a tissue out of her purse and wiped her index finger over and over. "Did you notice how *filthy* it was?" she said. "And don't tell me the children don't come down that hill. And she admitted they took Section Eight."

"That's a federal law," I reminded her. "If it's subsidized, they can't turn away people who are eligible. It was the same back in Illinois, if you recall."

Of course she did. "Remember that first place I lived? Where that disgusting woman who lived across the hall refused to take her medications?"

But not being "settled," or even close to it, was wearing on her, I could tell, and when we pulled in back at the camp, she said, "Why isn't there something like that in Waterville?"

"I don't know, Mom," I said, "but you have to order from the menu."

Her mouth tightened at this. I'd been saying it a lot lately.

THEN WE CAUGHT a break. Two of them, actually. During one of her trips that spring, Barbara had seen a house she loved, though it was too expensive. It was still available, and the price had come down a bit, but what really made it worth reconsidering was something we hadn't considered: taxes. We'd been warned by my Colby colleagues and just about everyone else, including realtors, that real-estate taxes here were brutally high. It hadn't occurred to us that people almost everywhere believe they're overtaxed—a belief particularly virulent in Maine. One afternoon, as an exercise, Barbara sat down with our realtor for the first time and actually ran the numbers on that house, only to discover that it wasn't completely out of our range and that, compared with Illinois, taxes in Maine were a bargain. True, you got less house for your dollar, but a smaller percentage of that dollar went to the state. The result was a push. Better still, now that the house had been on the market for almost two years, the sellers were thought to be motivated. What could it hurt to look? Given that love invariably enters through the eye, that was a dumb question. We looked, and of course it was the ideal house. Back at the realtor's we ran the numbers again with the same result. It would be a stretch, but not impossible. I called my literary agent to ask what kind of money we could reasonably anticipate in the coming year, then told the realtor we'd sleep on it and decide in the morning whether to make an offer or not. But by the time we got back to the lake, we'd changed our minds and called our realtor and instructed her to make an offer that would reveal if *motivated* meant the same thing to these sellers that it did to us a few months earlier in southern Illinois, when it had been synonymous with *desperate,* or *about to pray for the first time in twenty-five years.*

We might have guessed what effect our finally finding *the* house would have on my mother, but we didn't. My mantra— that come the end of the day, she was going to have to order off the menu—was an idea she'd always resisted. Usually she stood her ground, maintaining that we just had to keep looking, that there had to be something we simply hadn't found yet. And of course by *we* she meant me. But the journey from Illinois had taken more out of her than we knew, as had the repeated rental disappointments. Maine itself—the deep stillness of the woods, the piney dampness of the camp, the lonely sound of the loons out on the pond in the middle of the night—seemed to unmoor her; these rustic routines were ours, not hers, and she was increasingly desperate for control over some little corner of our present existence. One evening Barbara and I met a new colleague and his wife for dinner in nearby Bel- grade Lakes, leaving her and the girls alone at the camp for a couple hours. Emily and Kate were up in their beloved loft, headphones on as usual, listening to music and dancing. Their youthful exuberance must've been too much for my mother. Eventually, even with their headphones on, they heard her calling up to them from the bottom of the stairs, asking them to please keep the noise down. She was trying, she explained, to count her change.

The next day things came to a head. We'd been in nego- tiation all week with suddenly *un*motivated sellers who were playing things as if they had the stronger hand, which meant they did. They'd apparently heard that the bidder was a Colby College professor, and in a mill town like Waterville that was their dream come true. Worse, it was now early August, and classes would start in a few weeks. The sellers had no doubt also heard that we were out on Great Pond in an unheated camp that would be impossible to stay warm in past the end of September. To their way of thinking, we were like Napoléon. On impulse we'd invaded Russia, and winter was coming.

On the night in question, all five of us gathered around the camp's television with the sound down low so we could hear the phone if it rang. The patio door was open just a crack, because the nights were already chilly. Through the opening came a sound like paper being wadded into balls—but loud, as if played through a bullhorn. Orange light, for some reason, was dancing on the smooth surface of the lake. The camp two doors down from ours was ablaze, huge columns of fire soaring into the sky. All around the cove people had come out onto their decks to watch. When the fire leaped from the camp itself to the two nearest pine trees, I said, "Uh, I don't mean to be an alarmist, but let's get in the car and drive up to the main road." On foot, it would be an uphill climb along the dirt road, and my mother didn't do uphill anymore, even in broad daylight. There wasn't much of a breeze, but if it shifted in our direction, I'd have to carry her, leaving Barbara to attend to the girls. We'd all just piled into our cars when the fire trucks careened down the road, effectively trapping us in our drive. Along with the neighbors, we watched the building burn down to its foundation, the firefighters seemingly content to keep the flames from leaping from tree to tree and camp to camp. As often was the case with my mother, when faced with a real worry, some clear and present danger, she was remarkably calm, reassuring Kate and Emily that everything would be fine, that the firemen knew what they were doing.

The episode did, however, provide her with a valuable new context. "I've changed my mind about the Farmingdale apartment," she said the next morning over breakfast. "Let's take it."

I nodded, not wanting to queer the deal with excess enthusiasm. "Do you want to go look at it again?"

"No, I've decided."

"Are you sure?"

"Let's call her now," she said. "Then it'll be all settled." And after that, we could call the movers and set a date for the delivery of her things. She could start making out a grocery list.

"It looks like we might be getting the house we want," I told her (as we did, the day after). "You can stay with us for a while if you aren't sure," I said, feeling Barbara stiffen next to me. "We can keep looking."

"I'm sure," she said. "Let's call now."

Right now, she meant, right this *second*. Which was fine. I'd just needed to hear her say the words. Otherwise, when the Farmingdale apartment didn't work out (as it wouldn't), she'd remember it as being all my fault, and at the very least I had to make her complicit.

So we made the call. The apartment was still available. Yes, we could drive to Farmingdale later that morning with a deposit. And when we returned, we could start calling the telephone, cable, and utilities. That afternoon, when Barb and the girls were out, she called her sister in Gloversville to celebrate, describing the apartment in detail and how quiet the complex was—all elderly, no Section 8s—and how it sat on a hill overlooking the river. My aunt must have said it sounded perfect because I heard my mother agree, and of course she'd convinced herself that it was. "And the best part?" she added. "It's not just a new apartment. It's a new life."

By the time she hung up, she was aglow. "Oh, Ricko-Mio," she said, giving me a hug. "It feels so *good*. I don't know why it took me so long to decide."

That evening, though, she began to come down from her manic high. The movers had called, and it would be at least two weeks before they could deliver her things from Illinois. No, they couldn't give her a specific delivery date; the problem was she had so little that it would have to go on the back of a truck bound for New England with a larger load. And, of course, she'd begun to remember her original misgivings about the apartment. "Before we move in so much as a stick of furniture, the whole place will have to be professionally cleaned," she said. "Remember the layer of *grease* on that stove top?"

I considered saying no, since I didn't, then decided to agree that, yes, it had been greasy.

"It'll be worth the money," she continued, her conviction on this point unshakable. To the uninitiated, it no doubt would have appeared that it was her own she meant to spend.

Again I agreed, this time really meaning it. For the bargain price of a good cleaning, we'd be purchasing peace of mind. Temporary, yes, but no less necessary for that.

Unsettled

"THAT'S YOURS, you know," my mother said, startling me. She'd drifted off to sleep in her chair, and for the last hour I'd worked quietly, packing her books in preparation for yet another move. She was now living in Winslow, in her third apartment since we moved to Maine a decade earlier. How long had she been awake, observing me? I'd been listening to her low, regular breathing as I worked and hadn't noticed any change. I made a point of not watching my mother when she slept. Whereas other people relaxed in sleep, my mother's face always became rigid, a rictuslike mask, as if even in sleep she was doing battle with demons that would advance whenever her conscious guard was down. A month earlier she'd had another major meltdown, after which she'd slipped into one of the listless fugue states that so often followed a manic event. Coming out the other side, there was always a return to sanity, and at least for a time she'd rediscover her ability to see things as they were, her thoughts no longer barbed and dangerous. But this most recent meltdown seemed to have taken a greater toll than any of the others, and things we'd fought pitched battles over in the past seemed not to matter now. All of which was both welcome and a little unnerving, and all afternoon as I'd packed her books, my mother drifting in and out of sleep in her reading chair, I couldn't help wondering if something had finally broken inside her. I feared it might be her spirit. What made me almost physically ill to contemplate was that there'd been times when I'd secretly wished for precisely this, because it was her indomitable will that fueled this costly, unwinnable war, her intractable determination that was responsible for her seemingly endless suffering. Now, though, seeing her as listless and malleable as she'd been these last few weeks, I understood that this had been a mistake to hope for.

"I do wish you'd take it home with you," she sighed, referring to the copy of Anita Brookner's *Hotel du Lac* I'd just run across. I'd loaned her the book the year before, and at the time she'd claimed to like it, though when I offered other Brookners, she'd quickly said no, she didn't think so, there was so little room on her shelves.

Which was true enough, I thought, setting the novel aside. Her bookcases were crammed, many of the shelves double stacked. But of course there was more to it than that. I was forever buying or loaning her books I thought she might like, something at least entertaining enough to distract her from her growing list of physical ailments. She suffered crippling arthritis in her fingers, toes, and lower back. For this she took Aleve, which made her stomach feel like someone was clawing at it from the inside with a garden tool. She had acid reflux and high blood pressure and a thyroid condition, all three of which required medication, and she complained of her legs "locking up" when she had to walk uphill or for any distance. She was also suffering periodic TIAs, or ministrokes, that left her exhausted and afraid, the fear making another such event all the more likely. And even if there'd been a cure for these problems, it wouldn't address the relentless cycle of her anxieties, the feeling that the walls of her world were closing in.

Occasionally I'd pick a winner, something "in the tradition of" Agatha Christie or Margery Allingham or Mary Stewart or one of her other favorite authors, but mostly she'd read a few pages and declare that they were in the tradition of trash, of rip-offs, of a fast buck. The next time I visited they'd be sitting on the table by the front door, usually in a ziplock Baggie, to be donated to the next library book sale. As the Baggie suggested, the issue was contamination. My mother loved every single book on her sagging shelves, as they'd allowed her countless hours of escape. She didn't want them rubbing spines with books she deemed unworthy.

Which I kind of understood, and was why, despite having had to do it a dozen times or more, I never minded packing up her books for each subsequent move. My mother had what you could call a library. While there were fewer than five hundred books, almost all of them inexpensive paperbacks, some with printed prices as low as a quarter on them, they revealed her taste and personality. I had ten times as many but nothing like a library. My wife and I had combined our books long ago—our tastes mostly compatible if not identical—and many on our shelves were written by former students or colleagues. An astonishing number were advance readers' editions sent by publishers hoping for endorsements, and of course there were others that for one reason or another I felt obliged to read. Barbara and I both have a hard time disposing of books, even those we don't like, aware that behind even the most wretched failures there's an author who slaved lovingly, for who knows how long. That's a sentimental attitude, of course, and if you indulge it, you'll never have a real library, certainly not one like my mother's. If a stranger came into her apartment, a quick scan of her books would give him a pretty good idea of who she was, whereas all he could say about ours was, *Boy, these people sure have a lot of books.*

"Why don't you let me buy you another bookcase," I said, going back to work. "Your new apartment's bigger. I'm pretty sure there'd be room."

What I was really hoping to elicit was some kind of enthusiasm for her new place, though I was pretty sure no such remarks would be forthcoming. Her next apartment, in an assisted-living facility, was very expensive (though we'd concealed the cost from her) and upscale, and she hated everything about it: the cheery regimented activities, the noonday meal in the large dining room, the railings along every hallway (implying that everyone not on a walker would need to clutch onto these in order to keep upright), the van used to ferry residents to the supermarket and the doctor and the hairdresser (which she'd never take because "my son does all that"). We'd put her name on the list at several other housing complexes, but it wasn't moving up those lists fast enough, and she grew frustrated with me for not calling every few days to check. I explained this in effect meant I was asking if anyone had died or had been hospitalized or was feeling poorly, because illness and death were what created vacancies. So rather than wait, she'd decided on the assisted living she knew she'd hate, since at least she'd be settled.

"I don't want a new bookcase," she sighed. "I just want all this to be over."

The move, she meant, but maybe more than that.

"You don't have to go anywhere, Mom," I reminded her. "If it's too much, you can stay right here."

"We signed a lease."

"Those can be broken."

"You've hired movers. We've canceled the cable, the phone . . . everything."

"Yes, but we can undo all that."

She rubbed her temples. "Can we please, *please,* just not talk about this?"

The apartment in Farmingdale had lasted only a year. It was too far from Waterville, as I'd known it would be, even before I saw it. We'd tried to mitigate the distance by inviting her to dinner every week or so and including her in school plays and other activities involving her granddaughters, as well as college events like the annual Carols and Lights holiday festival. Most important, we strove for continuity by reestablishing our usual routines. Saturday was for grocery shopping, just as it had been in southern Illinois, after which she and I went out to lunch, something she always looked forward to. And of course we talked on the phone during the week. Still, she made no secret of how isolated she felt in Farmingdale, mostly from me but also from Emily and Kate, who were growing up fast. Though there were a lot of women her age in the Farmingdale complex, she'd made no friends there, claiming women from Maine were provincial and clannish and dull. They cared little for politics, less for sports, nothing at all for fashion. They liked their seafood fried and their pastries dense. They were sluggish and self-satisfied. They gossiped incessantly about people my mother didn't know, and they weren't interested in her opinions.

So when an apartment not far from our house in Waterville came on the market, Barbara and I immediately checked it out on our own. That way, if it was a sty, there was no reason to get her hopes up. But it was lovely, half of the downstairs of a large, rambling old house, and the landlord and his wife lived just up the street. About twice the size of the cramped Farmingdale place, it had high ceilings and tall windows, a fireplace, and a nice front porch for summer sitting. Naturally it was more expensive, but we were happy to make up the difference—or would have been if we thought she'd be happy there. Lovely, you see, is in the eye of the beholder, and Barbara was shaking her head in dismay. Over the years she'd grown almost as adept as I was at seeing things through my mother's eyes, and that's what she was doing now. The fixtures in the kitchen and bath were of the same vintage as those on Helwig Street in Gloversville, and the fridge wasn't frost-free. There were outlets in the unheated utility room for a washer and dryer, which my mother, a confirmed apartment dweller, didn't own. The beautiful oak built-ins would have to be dusted. Ditto the hardwood floors. My mother much preferred wall-to-wall carpeting, since you could run a vacuum over it.

"You think she'll hate it?" I asked.

"Not immediately. Not until after we sign the lease."

Which is pretty much how it had happened. A few days later, standing in the kitchen, the landlord and his wife awaiting our decision in the living room, she'd raised all the pertinent, predictable objections. Her back wouldn't allow her to defrost a refrigerator. (That was fine, we'd get her a new one.) And she had no way to get to a laundromat. (No problem, we'd scout out a nice used washer/dryer unit.) And she hated wood floors. (A few area rugs would do the trick.) Knowing what would come next, Barbara left the room. "And of course the whole place will need a *professional* cleaning," she said, sotto voce, drawing her index finger across the surface of the stove. "There's a layer of grease over everything." (From the next room came the voice of the landlord's wife, "*What* did she say?")

So we signed a lease and later, back at our house, my mother called Gloversville to tell my aunt about her lovely new place, how much it reminded her of the Helwig Street house, and how close she'd be to us. To hear her tell it, this move was really for me. I'd grown weary of the half-hour drive to Farmingdale to take her grocery shopping. Now we could shop together in Waterville, and she'd really be part of Emily's and Kate's lives again. Her enthusiasm, I knew, was more for herself than her sister. She was giving herself one of her talkings-to, convincing herself that she was doing the right thing, that all would at last be well.

For a while things *were* better, but then ultimately worse. It was an old house, so the tall windows, while elegant, didn't glide up and down smoothly on their fraying ropes, and the glass panes rattled when the wind blew or a big truck rumbled by. Summers, the street was too hot and noisy to sit out on the porch, or so she claimed. Her neighbors weren't elderly, which meant they made noise. The woman in the upstairs apartment was heavy-footed and played music, and on the other side of her bedroom wall my mother could hear the tenant in the adjacent apartment—a sad young woman—weeping inconsolably over a long-lost boyfriend. I visited regularly and never heard any of this, but the house *was* old and full of sounds.

There were other disappointments, too, unavoidable but real. Though she was closer to us now and saw her granddaughters more regularly, they were in middle and high school and had full lives with their friends. Barbara was by then working full-time at Colby College, and I was both writing and teaching, so even though she was now three minutes away instead of thirty, she didn't see ten times as much of us; the imagined arithmetic was false, as it always seemed to be where she was concerned. And now that she wasn't in a seniors' complex anymore, when she went to the mailbox there were no other women her age to talk to, even in passing, about the weather and who'd come down with a cold or had visitors over the weekend. When I called to check on her at the end of the day, she'd say, before hello, "Do you realize that yours is the first voice I've heard today that didn't come from the television?"

Then one day a bat came down the chimney, and that was that; we were off to Winslow, ten minutes away, on the other side of the Kennebec River, where I'd been tracking a small elderly housing complex, and finally our timing was right. Truthfully, we hadn't expected this apartment to work out either, but it did, largely because my mother, against all odds, had made a friend there, a woman her age, also "from away" and therefore unattached. Dot was kind and had a terrific sense of humor and also seemed to have the great reserves of patience this friendship would require. She had family down-state, though, and sometimes spoke about moving to be closer to them, talk that always sent my mother into a tizzy.

Dot was one of my many reasons for feeling particularly dubious about this upcoming move. I was more than willing to make the weekly drive from the coast to take my mother grocery shopping and out to lunch and wherever else she needed to go. Some weeks, if she had a doctor's appointment, I might have to make the trip twice, a strain, sure, but doable. And of course we could talk on the phone as needed. There was no guarantee she would find somebody she liked as well as Dot in her new place. But my mother believed she could read the future. If she remained in Winslow, Dot would leave, and then she'd be alone. Okay, I said, but wouldn't *that* be the time to move? Why not enjoy her friend for as long as she could? Because, I was given to understand, if there was the possibility of moving in the future, that would mean she was unsettled in the present. No, she'd just go. If she didn't find another friend, well, she'd do without.

"There," I said, taping the last of the boxes shut. "Done."

"You should go home," she said, offering up one of her despondent smiles. "You have responsibilities there."

"Mom. We're going to walk away from this," I reminded her. "I'll be here an hour before the movers. We let them in, and then we drive away. They're going to pack everything here and unpack it at the other end."

This new moving strategy was one I'd expected her to challenge me on. In the past she'd insisted on being present for both the loading and unloading, as if her physical presence and attention to the smallest details would prevent damage to objects that, once put in their proper and accustomed place, would reconstitute her small interior world. The resulting spike in her anxiety levels in the weeks prior to a move made her impossible to live with, and naturally she'd be wiped out for weeks afterward, too tired and worn out even to eat. Over the last few years she'd become wobbly, unsteady on her feet (in need, actually, of the wall railings her new place boasted). Always managing to position herself in doorways when the movers, carrying something heavy or fragile, were trying to get through, she was a danger to both herself and them. And if anything got dirty or scuffed on the truck, she'd squeal in horror at the smudge and demand that it be cleaned then and there, before it entered the apartment, so everything came to a screeching halt. The placement of every stick of furniture was a battle in itself, and common sense was not allowed onto the battlefield. If the cable plug was on one wall, she'd invariably want her television by the opposite one, requiring the cable company to send out a technician to provide a second outlet. No feng shui enthusiast could take more seriously the arrangement of a bedroom, which had to "feel" right to her, irrespective of function. If there were only two electrical outlets in the room, you could rest assured of my mother's intention to cover them, after which another electrician would have to be hired.

I was determined to avoid all of this unnecessary angst by getting her out of the Winslow apartment the moment the movers arrived, establishing her at our Camden house for the day until her things were off-loaded at the new apartment. Toward that end I'd drawn a schematic of her new place and asked her to decide where the major pieces of furniture should go, promising she wouldn't be held to any decisions and that anything could be repositioned later if need be.

"Really," I reassured her. "There's nothing for you to do. Nothing for you to worry about. Call me if anything comes up."

But I only had to look at her to know that her imagination was already running wild. What if they cut off her utilities too early? What if she couldn't reach me? What if, what if, what if?

"Would you rather come to Camden with me now?"

"Dot and I are going to the Lobster Trap. Did you forget?"

"No, I didn't forget," I assured her. "I know you've been looking forward to it. I was just offering. I'll call you tomorrow. We can talk everything through again if you'd like to. Absolutely nothing's going to go wrong."

I was halfway to the car when her door opened behind me, and I heard her calling out. "What?" I said, turning back. She was holding up the Anita Brookner. See? I forgot things. I'd forgotten that, at least. Things *could* go wrong.

In fact, though she didn't say so, everything *was* going wrong.

HER MOST RECENT MELTDOWN had been occasioned by a number of related factors that could be reduced to this: our lives were changing. Buoyed by the success of the movie Robert Benton made of my novel *Nobody's Fool* and some screenplay opportunities, I'd resigned my position at Colby College to write full-time, a decision that struck my mother as both rash and dangerous. Two decades earlier she'd felt much the same way about my out-of-the-blue determination to become a novelist, an act of hubris, she thought, that threatened my stable career as an English professor. My recent successes as a writer were tangible, but to her they remained utterly baffling. She read each glowing review with genuine pride, often tearing up, and reveled in the modest regional prizes my books garnered. If she'd had the money, she no doubt would've hired contract killers to settle the score with critics who had the temerity to doubt my brilliance. After the *Nobody's Fool* movie, the novel itself made a cameo appearance on the *New York Times* best-seller list, which threw her for a loop. "It's like it's all happening to someone else" was how she put it, and I sympathized because it mostly felt that way to me, too.

From various comments she let drop, I knew she was deeply mystified by how many people apparently wanted to read stories set in the kind of industrial backwaters from which she'd worked so hard to escape. Even more perplexing was the fact that I not only wrote about such places but returned to them again and again. After all, I had a Ph.D. and a valid passport and made a good living among distinguished colleagues. Why was I slumming (imaginatively) back in Gloversville? She probably felt quite certain that in short order people would decide they'd had enough of stories set in dirty mill towns, and if I quit my job, where would I be?

The success of my fiction gravely conflicted with her own experience of life, as well as her profound sense of how the world went round. After all, she'd grown up during the Depression. My teaching position to her felt every bit as solid as the college that employed me. If Colby wasn't going anywhere and my tenure couldn't be revoked, then I was set for life or, to use her word, *settled*. Why court disaster by exposing myself to unnecessary risk? Why *choose* to be unsettled? As things stood I got a good paycheck every two weeks, whereas an author's life would be one of feast or famine. Its feasts not only were unpredictable but came intertwined with all kinds of whens and ifs—like, *if* you can finish the book you're working on, *when* you can deliver it—and such uncertainties were dry tinder, lacking only a spark to ignite a conflagration. We already had one daughter in college, and the other would soon follow. Could we cover those heart-stopping expenses by means of my writing alone? I assured her that we could and tried to explain that at least for the moment my being a teacher was actually counterproductive, that the time I spent in the classroom diminished rather than increased my earning power, but that didn't register. To her, resigning my teaching position wasn't just folly but a particular kind of folly of which she had personal knowledge. Forty years before, on a whim, she'd quit a good job, and look what that had gotten her.

And it went even deeper than this. One of my mother's most cherished convictions was that back on Helwig Street she and I had pledged an oath, each to the other. She and I would stand together against whatever configuration the world's opposition took—her parents, my father, Gloversville, monetary setbacks. Now, forty-some years later, I was a grown man with a wife and kids, but this original bond, she believed, was still in force. However fond she was of Barbara, however much she loved her granddaughters, none of that altered our original contract, which to her way of thinking made us indivisible. She'd never really considered us two separate people but rather one entity, oddly cleaved by time and gender, like fraternal twins somehow born twenty-five years apart, destined in some strange way to share a common destiny. If I was about to make a colossal blunder, then it was her duty, her moral obligation, to prevent it. Having been prideful herself, she knew what pride goeth before. What's more, my pride was risking not just my own future but my family's, putting them and, yes, herself in unnecessary danger. Because when things came unraveled, a son who at times failed to acknowledge the primacy of the Helwig Street contract might, if there weren't enough resources to go around, put his wife and children before her. I don't think these were conclusions my mother arrived at in the front of her brain; instead they were constant, ambient whisperings that originated in the shadowy recesses, as undeniably real as anything in the world for the simple reason that they never, even in jaw-clenched sleep, went away.

STILL, MY MOTHER MIGHT have been able to give herself a good talking-to and keep the worst of these anxieties at bay had I not compounded matters by announcing, not long after quitting my teaching job, our plan to move to the coast. Not that she didn't understand the logic. Now that I was untethered to the college, there was nothing holding us in Waterville. A few years earlier, we'd purchased a condo in Camden that we used as a weekend and summer retreat. It was three stories tall, one full quarter of a former Methodist church. Our unit was beneath the smaller of the two steeples, a place full of light and air, especially the master bedroom on the top floor, from which we had a view of the harbor. Barbara and I both loved it there but finally had to admit that it just wasn't working out. For one thing, our girls were then in high school and hated being yanked away from their Waterville friends and activities. For another, though she never said so in so many words, our having the place in Camden put my mother out of sorts. If we spent the weekend there, I'd have to take her grocery shopping on Friday instead of Saturday, our long-established grocery day. And in the summer, though we frequently invited her to come along, she felt abandoned. She liked Camden itself, its shops and restaurants a vivid contrast to dark, moribund Waterville, but the hills, so beautiful to look at, frustrated and defeated her. All the places she wanted to go were within a hundred yards of our front door, but at the bottom of the slope. She had no trouble going down it, but once there she couldn't make her legs carry her back up again, which meant that whoever she was with would have to return home for the car. With the part of her brain that was rational and reasonable, she understood our preference for bright, vibrant Camden; the irrational, fearful part, however, harbored a suspicion that we'd purposely selected a place where she couldn't follow or, if she did, couldn't function. This was precisely the sort of paradox she was forever trying and failing to reconcile. On the one hand, we'd never once in thirty-five years abandoned her. On the other, we always appeared to be on the verge of doing so.

Moreover, the worst of her personal demons was the one who dwelt in the details, and this was especially true of our plan to move to the coast. Had we been able to give her a series of dates etched in stone—for selling the Waterville house, finding a new house in Camden, locating her new apartment, and the actual physical moves themselves—she could have written them on her calendar and checked them off, one by one, the way her mother had always done with Holy Days on the liturgical calendar. But we could offer nothing that was "for sure." Because property was more expensive on the coast, there was a real possibility we wouldn't be able to find or afford what we were looking for—but then again maybe we'd get lucky! To further complicate matters, after a couple of mills around Waterville closed, half the town was for sale, which guaranteed that unloading our house—something we needed to do in order to buy in Camden—was going to be tricky.

And these were just the surface complexities. Supposing we found a new place and managed to sell the old one, what would happen next? We couldn't say with any certainty. Normally her need to be settled, to reestablish her old routines in a fresh environment, would have been trump, but there were simply too many moving parts to accurately predict how things would go. If we rented an apartment on the coast and moved her in, it might be six months or a year before we could follow, and there was no chance she'd make it that long in a strange place, with us a good hour away. If *we* went first, there was the possibility of a similar gap before she could follow, because senior housing here was as problematic as it had been in Waterville. And while there were more options, they were all more expensive, so she'd be more financially dependent on us. And every place we looked into had a waiting list. How long would you have to wait for an apartment in a complex of twelve units if there were three people ahead of you? Or eight people in one of twenty-five? The answer to both questions was the same: as long as it took. If she put her name on the list too soon and an apartment came available before she was ready, what then?

We'd presented her with a Rubik's Cube of possibility, the very thing we should have known she couldn't handle. The best we could do was to assure her that we'd take care of everything when the time came. Meanwhile she only needed to be patient. It was a doomed strategy, but it was the only one we had. It was either that or . . .

Over the last thirty-five years, my wife and I had taken turns bringing up the inevitable *or*. This time it was Barbara's. We *did* have a choice, she reminded me. Either we asked my mother to live with things being unsettled until we could settle them, *or* we could just put our own lives on hold. We didn't *have* to move to the coast to be happy. I'd quit my job at Colby, but Barbara was still employed there and liked her job. We didn't *need* to move; we just wanted to. The question we had to articulate correctly and then answer carefully was the same one we'd confronted so often before. In the end, was doing what we wanted to do—what other people like us seemed to do without having to think about it—really worth it? Was the reward equal to the risk? My mother was no longer a young woman, and her health was clearly in decline. Even though we'd managed her last two moves—both of which she'd instigated—as much as she'd allowed us, it had taken her long months to recover from them. Another move—this one played under protest—might just do her in. Why not put everything on hold?

To this persuasive argument I had a one-word answer: genetics. Yes, my mother's health was in decline, but my grandmother had also suffered from high blood pressure, a thyroid condition, crippling arthritis, and ministrokes, and she lived into her nineties, as had her sisters. By contrast, my father hadn't made it to his sixty-fifth birthday, and neither had a couple of his brothers, nor had Barbara's parents. If my mother lived to be ninety, we'd be in our early sixties before we were allowed to make unencumbered decisions about our own lives. I was a Russo male, a bloodline ripe with its own genetic challenges, cancer primary among them. Add to this the environmental issue: I'd grown up in Gloversville, where cancer statistics soared off the actuarial charts. If my mother lived to be ninety, odds were good she'd outlive me. When I spoke with my cousin Greg on the phone and inquired after my aunt's health, he always joked that these old women—his mother and mine—were going to bury us both. Except it wasn't a joke. When in the last thirty-five years, I asked my wife, had we ever had the luxury of making a major decision purely on its merits? Of necessity we'd always had to consider my mother's needs before our own. Surely by now we'd earned a reprieve. Didn't we deserve the right to think about ourselves first for once? It wasn't as if we were planning to abandon her. We would find her a nice place to live, just as we'd always done. We'd pay for what she couldn't afford and make the move as stress-free as possible.

I was right, of course, and Barbara admitted as much. After all, she'd been throwing the same argument at me for more than thirty years, every time it was my turn to raise the dreaded *or*. The problem was that I was also wrong, and we both knew that, too. Nor was I surprised when she remembered my grandfather. "What was that saying of his?" she asked. He'd always been full of aphorisms, but I knew all too well the one she was referring to. "With your grandmother, you always have a choice," he was fond of remarking when I was a boy. "You can do things her way or you can wish you had." He was speaking about his wife, of course, but he might have been talking about his strong-willed daughter. By the end, he was.

THE HOUSE WE ENDED UP buying in Camden was old and elegant. Also, a potential money pit. In its most recent incarnation it had devolved into a three-family dwelling. The principal renters had lived on the ground floor in the main house, where there was a master suite with a lovely bathroom. On the second floor were two more small bedrooms, as well as a tiny apartment with its own entrance. At some point a large garage had been added at the back of the house and, above it, a second, larger apartment with a third-story loft. It wasn't a house we were originally interested in, but Chris, our realtor, knew I was a writer and thought the loft apartment over the garage would be a perfect workspace for me. "And if you fix up the little apartment," he added, "it might work for your mom." Early on we'd told him what we were up against, that in addition to selling our Waterville house and finding something we could afford in Camden, we'd also need to find a place for my mother, and he'd promised to keep an eye out for a one-bedroom apartment.

"Or not," he said with a smile, seeing that his helpful suggestion had caused all the blood to drain from Barbara's face. An observant breed, realtors. My wife would later become one.

Chris was right about the loft workspace, though, and while the main house needed a lot of work, it was pretty much what we were looking for. The wiring wasn't up to code, a costly fix, and the kitchen was mired in the Sixties. Many of the windows needed to be replaced. The real problem, however, was the tiny run-down apartment. We had no interest in renting it, so what on earth would we do, pretend it didn't exist? On the other hand, it was one of the reasons the house was in our price range. The property had been on the market for years and, according to the seller's agent, most prospective buyers were put off by the three-family arrangement. Eventually, he thought, it would sell to an investor who'd fix up and rent all three spaces. Because of the apartment the house was definitely wrong for us, but there was something right about it, too, something that made me not want to dismiss it out of hand. Maybe it was just that we'd been looking for months and coming up empty. At any rate, I suggested we go up and look at that apartment one more time on the theory that if we considered the house at its worst, we'd feel better about turning our backs on what we liked.

You entered the apartment through the kitchen, and right away you thought, *No, no,* and again, *no.* The appliances were old and so grungy I immediately imagined my mother running her index finger along the surface of the stove. The stained, cracking linoleum was coming up from the floor. The living room was low ceilinged and so small it would hold little more than a sofa and coffee table, maybe a small TV in the corner. The bedroom was the size of a walk-in closet, with room for a single bed with one bedside table or a double bed without. In the bathroom, when you sat on the toilet your knees would touch the shower on one side, the wall on the other. The only good feature was the large and lovely screened-in porch that overlooked the back patio. I went out and just stood there. In winter, you'd glimpse the ocean through the bare trees. In summers I could imagine us sitting out there reading, cooled by breezes off the water. Sweet.

Barbara and Chris were in the hot little apartment waiting for me to come to my senses so we could leave. When I stepped inside, I got a flash. "What you're standing in," I said to Barbara, "is our master bedroom."

Chris blinked. My wife frowned. Whose master bedroom? Not hers. Not by a long shot.

But in a heartbeat I saw she was with me, seeing in her mind's eye what I was seeing in mine, and before I was half finished explaining, she was already ahead of me. You'd tear out the kitchen, knock down the wall that separated it from the living room, as well as the one between the bedroom and the bath. With its four tiny rooms reduced to two, the apartment could become a reasonably luxurious suite with its own private porch. Chris was grinning at us. "Moments like this," he said, "are why I'm a realtor."

Instead of returning to Waterville as planned, we booked a room at a B&B, and over dinner and a bottle of wine at the local chowder house we ran the numbers, trying to contain our mounting, irrational excitement, then ran them again. It was impossible. We could afford either the property or the work needed to transform it, but not both. Not unless we did all these things over a period of years. Not unless we moved into the loft apartment over the garage while the work was being done on the main house. Not unless I sold another screenplay. Not unless we sold the Waterville house, which after a month on the market still hadn't generated a single showing. Not unless we could find an apartment nearby for my mother. We'd have to hire a structural engineer to make sure the walls we meant to tear down weren't load bearing, and we'd have to bring the girls to see if this was a house they could see themselves returning to in the future with children of their own. Yet somehow, in the moment when we'd seen how it might be done, how the house's many drawbacks could be transformed into a real asset, we'd already bought it in our imaginations. Impossible had become something we'd just have to deal with.

And my mother? Well, she hadn't come into our thinking at all, not until we came home late one evening not long afterward to find a message from her on the answering machine, telling me to call the minute I got back, no matter what time. Okay, I thought, this is it. Now we pay. I dialed her number.

She answered on the first ring. She'd been thinking about it for a long time, she told me, her voice rich with both challenge and mania, and had come to an important decision. She was going home.

RETURNING TO GLOVERSVILLE yet again might have been a lunatic notion, but it was hardly a new one. The idea began to take form, as near as I could tell, in the camp we rented when we first came to Maine, after which it advanced and receded according to the cycles of her mind. The problem (and I'd been aware of this since she and I made that first journey to Arizona) was that to my mother there were two Gloversvilles—the one she was always trying to escape from when she lived there, and the other she nostalgically considered, every time she fled, as home. When she was actually in residence, it was a small, insular, uncouth, narrow-minded place that prevented her from being her truest self—free spirited, unconventional, and unfettered. Once she'd flown the coop, though, the very qualities she detested became more attractive. The smallness she so despised became cozy; it meant you didn't need a car to live there. Your loved ones, the very people who intruded upon your privacy and always spouted unwanted advice, were a convenient block away. Seen from a distance, they weren't so much nosy as thoughtful and caring, their concern now a safety net.

What took me longer to understand was that just as there were two Gloversvilles, my mother also had two sisters. In reality, she and Phyllis couldn't have been more temperamentally different, and when my mother was living there it was always their differences that defined their relationship. She saw my aunt as conventional and interfering and judgmental, qualities Phyllis inherited, she thought, from their mother. There were many bones of contention, but it particularly infuriated my mother that neither her sister nor the local man she married, my uncle Mick, seemed to have any aspirations beyond the town line. To my uncle, who'd grown up on a farm and been too young to serve in World War II, Gloversville was the big city, and he made no secret of his affection for it. Their oldest son, Greg, my cousin and boyhood friend, had gone away to college but returned to marry a local girl and settled down to a life of deflated Fulton county wages. He and his wife lived next door to my aunt and uncle, and next door to them lived Mick's mother, Beatrice, for whom my mother had even less use than her son. That three generations were all living in the same block struck my mother, back when she'd returned to live on Helwig Street with my grandmother, as beyond perverse. They all walked into one another's homes without knocking, freely investigating the contents of the refrigerators and helping themselves without permission. Lacking even the most rudimentary notion of privacy, they saw no reason not to comment on everyone else's lives and day-to-day decisions. Who could bear to live like this?

Once away from Gloversville, however, my mother immediately saw things differently, and as she grew older, her nostalgia for the very proximity that had always stifled her so became more pronounced. "How *happy* we were on Helwig Street," she'd recall, her eyes misty with memory, as if we'd been cruelly banished from this Eden. "We didn't have much money," she'd concede, somehow imagining this had been the only impediment to our contentment, "but everything seemed so *safe*. Remember how we used to rap on the floor?" I did indeed. When we wanted to parlay with my grandparents or they with us, we would rap on the kitchen floor (they on the ceiling) with a broom handle, and we'd convene invisibly, but close enough to whisper—in the back hallway. At the time I regarded the broom handle as one of the many advantages to our upstairs/downstairs circumstances and assumed everyone would be envious to know how easily and efficiently we communicated, with no need even to pick up a phone. Whereas my mother always cited this broom knocking as an example of how much better our lives would be when we finally escaped Helwig Street. We'd be independent, she explained, without people beneath us who at their every whim felt entitled to so rudely summon us.

When rational, she knew returning to Gloversville was a pipe dream, but desperation had a way of transforming every image projected in the theater of her mind, neither vague nor cloudy, as you might expect, but in brilliant high definition. Maine was all muted sepia tones, whereas Helwig Street—and Sixth Avenue, where her sister lived—seemed close enough to touch, everything painted in bright primary colors. Just as vivid in her imagination was the self she would become once she returned home. In Gloversville, she wouldn't be pushing eighty. She'd be the age she was during her last stint, when my grandmother was still alive. To be sure, she hadn't been in the best of health even then, but she'd managed well enough and would again.

She'd only been in that first Farmingdale apartment a few

months before she floated the idea of moving home again. It was a Saturday afternoon, after we'd done the grocery shopping, and we were watching a ball game before I headed back to Waterville. She'd been out of sorts the whole time.

"We might as well face facts," she finally said. "I hate Maine. I never should've come here." I had to smile, given how she made it sound like she'd done it all on her own. "It was a mistake. I should've gone straight to Gloversville from Illinois. I don't know what I was thinking."

"Okay," I said, "but while we're facing facts, here's another. You also hate Gloversville. You have your whole life. The last time you went back there, it was—in your own words—a terrible mistake."

There were few things my mother liked less than having such statements thrown back at her, so this put her into a dark funk. "It's true I've always hated Gloversville," she conceded half an hour later when the game ended and I rose to leave, "but things there have changed."

Which was true. They'd become even more problematic. In the past she'd always had the Helwig Street house, but that had been sold, in part to pay for the long-term care my grandmother required toward the end of her life. What my mother was referring to, however, was that my aunt and uncle had swapped houses with my cousin Greg and his wife, Carole, who had two kids and needed the extra room. Phyllis and Mick now occupied the downstairs flat of the house next door. My mother's idea, it finally came out, was for them to evict their upstairs renters so she could move in. "I'd have some kind of life there, at least," she concluded. "Aren't I entitled to that much?"

"Are you forgetting you can't do stairs anymore?" I couldn't help pointing out. After all, this consideration had governed every apartment search we'd made since Illinois. Indeed, when she visited our house these days, all activities had to take place on the ground floor because the pitch of the stairs up to the girls' bedroom was too steep. "I could *there*," she said, her stony expression daring contradiction. "You forget. I always lived on the second floor in Gloversville."

In fact, she went on, nothing was really wrong except *Maine*. Once back in Gloversville she'd not only feel better, she'd *be* better. Why? Because there she'd at least be a person. Her family would be close by, along with other people who'd known her all her life, who knew she was a human being, who believed not only in her but also in her resilience and her ability to accomplish things. In Maine, none of the above.

I didn't see any point in debating whether she'd be more of a person in Gloversville than Camden, so I moved on to other problematic specifics, though I was pretty sure this tactic would prove equally futile. "How would you do your groceries? How would you get to the doctor or the hairdresser?"

"Greg would take me."

"Greg's juggling three jobs, and Carole works all week at the bank."

"Then I'd go with Mick and Phyl."

"Except you like to hold to your own schedule. Remember how you always complained, when you and Grandma lived together, that every week there'd be a different grocery day? They'd call and tell you to be ready in five minutes, and forty-five minutes later you'd still be waiting? How would that be different now? Have they changed? Have you?"

Her mouth had formed a thin line. "I'd *walk* to the store if I had to."

"In winter?"

Yes, she insisted, even in winter. Furthermore, if I was worried about money, there was no need. She'd get a job.

Of course I knew these wild assertions were trial balloons whose credibility she had to test by letting them float away, and that despite the brazenness of this last balloon—that she'd get a job—even she knew it would never gain altitude, no matter how much heated conviction she pumped into it.

"Mom," I said, "I'm not trying to make you feel bad, but we can't make real-world decisions based on magical thinking."

She was silent for a while, her face a dark thundercloud. "If only you wouldn't disagree with every single thing I say," she told me. "You take such pleasure in shooting down any idea I ever have. Why can't you be on *my* side for once?"

"What exactly would you like me to agree with?"

She thought for a moment. "That Greg would take me shopping. He's my nephew and he loves me."

"Yes, he would, and of course he does. That's why it would be so wrong to ask him to. He has too many other responsibilities and too few resources. The last thing he needs is another burden."

Now she threw me a triumphant look, as if this was the

concession she'd wanted from the start. "That's all I am, then? A burden? Is that what you're saying?"

"No, I'm saying that getting you to the hairdresser is my responsibility, not Greg's."

"Fine," she said. "Then I guess I'll just have to stay here in my cage."

The next day she called to apologize. After I left, she'd given herself a good talking-to. Her problem, she'd concluded, was always the same. She wanted to be independent, no one's burden or responsibility, not even mine. I had a career and a wife and two daughters to raise, and she hated that on top of all that I also had to think about her. She didn't know why her thoughts always returned to Gloversville, as if it were Briga-doon. She knew better. In the future, I was to simply ignore her when she "got like that."

The trouble, as she knew full well, was that when she got like that there *was* no ignoring her. Since then we'd been through the same bitter, futile exercise twice more, the volume turned up a notch or two each time. Now, on the eve of our move to the coast, we were back in familiar territory yet again, the only difference being that this time her fury was exagger-ated by further changes in the Gloversville landscape. Earlier that year my uncle Mick had died after a long, terrible illness, leaving my aunt hollowed out by grief and by the guilty relief that comes when a loved one's suffering finally ends. She and my mother had begun talking on the phone more regularly, usually once a week, usually reminiscing about their girlhoods on West Fulton Street, one of Gloversville's many immigrant neighborhoods. I think they both enjoyed these strolls down memory lane, and their nostalgia for simpler times made it easy to paper over their many ideological and temperamental differences. Lately, though, according to my aunt, with whom I also spoke regularly, my mother's mood had grown darker, as if she no longer had access even to the pleasures of the past, and the last time Phyllis asked her how things were going in the present, she said that there wasn't much point in talking about it, that she had no life, and there was no reason to pretend she did. Hearing this, my aunt called to warn me that another storm was approaching.

I, of course, needed no such warning. I'd seeded the clouds myself by ignoring my wife's *or* and sticking that FOR SALE sign in the yard in front of our Waterville house. Still, when the storm finally broke, even I was stunned by its ferocity. This time instead of telling me what she *wanted* to do, she was announcing what she *intended* to do, with or without my help. Having already been through the whole Gloversville scenario, she knew all my objections by heart and had no intention of listening to them again. She wasn't a child who needed to be told what she could and couldn't do. She was *going,* and that's all there was to it. There was nothing I could do to prevent it. If I didn't want to pay the movers, she'd leave every single thing she owned behind. If I wouldn't drive her there, she'd take a bus. If I wouldn't drive her to the bus, she'd take a taxi. Gloversville was where she belonged. She was going.

"Okay," I said, "but where specifically?" I knew, of course. My uncle's death meant that my aunt was now living alone in the two-bedroom downstairs flat, and it was that second bedroom my mother had in mind.

"Where do you think? With my sister."

The last thing I wanted was to ask the obvious question, but there was no avoiding it. "She's invited you?" I said.

This question was so cruel because I already knew the answer. My aunt had told me more than once that she was unsure whether she'd be staying in Gloversville much longer. Both of her daughters had asked her to come live with them, and she thought she might. I wondered now if she'd maybe mentioned this possibility to my mother, if perhaps that was what had precipitated the current meltdown. Because if Phyllis meant to move away, then my mother's final refuge, her last desperate hope for the independent life that existed nowhere except in her imagination, was disappearing before her eyes.

"What do you *mean,* has she invited me?" she demanded to know. "What are you *saying?*" But before I could explain that I wasn't *saying* anything, merely asking something, she continued, her voice now shaking with rage. "Are you actually implying that my sister would refuse to take me in?"

I took a deep breath and lowered my voice, hoping to balance her frenzy with calm and reason, though in truth I'd never known this strategy (or any other, for that matter) to work when she came totally unglued. "I'm saying your sister recently lost her husband. I'm saying she's raw with grief and unsure in her own mind what comes next."

"You know," my mother said, "it's all finally coming clear."

"What's that?"

"What you think of me. What you've always thought of me."

"Mom—"

"Did it ever occur to you," she wanted to know, "that maybe I could *help* my grieving sister? That there might be somebody in the world who actually likes me? As a person? Who might enjoy my company? That instead of being a burden—like I am to you—I might actually make someone's life better?"

"Mom—"

"Why don't you come right out and say it. You think I'm incapable of happiness. That I'm incapable of making anyone else happy."

To my surprise, I heard myself say, with a sinking heart, "All right, Mom. You win. Call Aunt Phyl. If Gloversville's what you want, I won't stand in your way."

The immediate and profound silence on the other end of the line suggested that I wasn't the only one surprised by this. She'd been prepared for several more rounds of verbal bludgeoning, but now she had to improvise. "As you say," I told her, "you're not a child."

After hanging up, I called my aunt and gave her the short version of what had just transpired. "Oh, poor Jean," she said.

"Yes," I said, immediately choked up that she could so perfectly sum up her sister's plight in three small words, and suddenly I felt both the weight and truth of the bitter questions my mother had just hurled at me. Had I considered even for an instant that she might be able to help her sister in her grief and loss? Had it occurred to me that my aunt might actually enjoy her company? That there actually might be someone, somewhere, who wouldn't see her as a burden? That there might be a place for her, a life? Because the honest answer to all those questions was a resounding no. No, nothing like that had crossed my mind. Worse, the real reason I was now calling my aunt was to apologize for the fact that my mother, who'd more than once accused me of trying to keep her in a cage, had broken out. Now Phyllis, whom I wanted to spare, was going to have a difficult morning.

"She keeps saying she wants to be with her family," I explained, "with people who love her."

"But *you* are her family," my aunt said. "You and Barbara and the girls."

"I know."

"It would cost you thousands to get her here, and two months later you'd have to bring her back again."

"I know," I repeated weakly.

"Oh, honey, I'm so sorry. And after all you've done . . . all these years. I wish I knew what to tell you."

"I wish you did, too."

We were silent for a time. "How's Barbara?"

"At the end of her tether," I admitted, grateful to have my wife, who'd borne all of this so patiently for three long decades, finally acknowledged. "Still here. Though, honestly, I can't imagine why."

"I feel so bad for her."

Suddenly I was anxious for the conversation to be over. You couldn't ask for a better confidante than my aunt, but I always felt like our shared understanding of my mother's condition, "her nerves," amounted to a shabby conspiracy against a sick woman, and I suspected Phyllis felt all too keenly that same sense of betrayal. And perhaps most unforgivable was that telephoning my aunt this evening, to prepare her for the call she'd be getting in the morning, constituted poisoning the well in advance of my mother's thirsty arrival.

That must've happened near the crack of dawn, because it was still very early when our telephone rang, waking us up. "Well, it's over," my mother said, not bothering with hello. "I guess I'm not going anywhere."

"I'm sorry, Mom," I told her, but she'd already hung up.

I lay there in bed for a long time, trying to imagine that terrible conversation with my aunt, who would've told her, as gently as possible, that what she was proposing simply wouldn't work, that most likely she wouldn't be staying in Gloversville that much longer herself, that by the end of the year she'd be putting the house on the market for what little it would bring, that after sorting things out she'd probably move in with one of her daughters. Knowing my aunt, I suspect she put in a good word on my behalf, reminding my mother that I loved her, that I'd always been there when she needed me, that she belonged close by so I could look after her, that she was lucky to have a son willing to do all that.

At some point another possibility occurred to me: that my mother hadn't called her sister at all, that all this was just between us, as it had always been. Locked in a two-person drama, we had no need for additional players.

BUILDING FLOOR-TO-CEILING SHELVES in the downstairs bedroom, which would double as a library and reading room when we didn't have guests, was the first order of business in the new Camden house. We'd hired a carpenter to begin work the day after the closing. "This whole wall?" he said dubiously, convinced we were nuts once we explained what we had in mind. After all, the living room already had ceiling-height bookcases, and the wall in question was very long indeed. Nobody had *that* many books. When we assured him we knew what we were doing, he reluctantly agreed, as if it were a bathroom he was remodeling and we'd instructed him to install three toilets, side by side. "As long as you won't get mad at me."

In a sense the carpenter had been right. We *had* badly misjudged—by underestimating what we needed. I'd forgotten that in addition to Barbara's and mine from the Waterville house there were all the books from my office at Colby College. We'd unpacked the books onto the new shelves hurriedly, almost helter-skelter, figuring that later we could rearrange them at our leisure and make sure Dickens and Trollope and Austen were comfortably rubbing spines and that Hammett and Chandler and James M. Cain and Ross Macdonald were in close enough proximity to swap soft-spoken, tough-guy lies after lights-out. Returning from Winslow after packing my mother's books, I collapsed, *Hotel du Lac* in hand, into a chair in the living room, too exhausted to do anything but stare at the wall of my own books, as well as the impressive pyramid of those that remained boxed and stacked right up to the ceiling in the corner. I counted these, trying to gauge how many additional bookcases would be required, where on the coast of Maine we'd find them, when there'd be time to look, and where we'd put them, but it had been a long day and I was far too tired to solve a problem with so many moving parts. I even was too worn out to roust myself from the chair and locate the shelf that contained the other Anita Brookners. Possibly they were still in one of those side boxes. Sitting there utterly drained, I wondered if maybe I was slipping into a funk of my own. Over the years I'd noticed that I was susceptible to my mother's moods, especially after spending a fair amount of time in her company. It was something I had to be careful of, because her periods of irrationality and dark depression had a tendency to infect both my writing and family life. I'd expected to feel better as soon as I got home, but instead, for some reason, I felt worse. Staring at all those books, shelved or not, I suddenly felt something akin to the anxiety—dread, really—that I knew my mother was prey to when her routines were in disarray.

One of her most cherished (and to my mind absurd) convictions had always been that she and I were essentially the same. If we didn't always see eye to eye, that was because I was twenty-five years younger; given time, I'd surely come around. Furthermore, at the heart of our most serious disagreements, she believed, was our fundamental similarity—our magnetic poles in effect repelling each other. I'd long imagined that she developed this ridiculous theory in order to explain to herself how she could have brought into the world a kid who couldn't have been more different from her if he'd been a foundling. But what if she was right? Was I really so different? In this respect her relationship to her own mother—a woman she considered conventional and moralistic and repressed—was illustrative. On the one hand there was no denying the two women agreed about virtually nothing, but there were some truly eerie temperamental similarities. One of my most vivid early memories of my grandmother had to do with her ongoing battles with milk. She preferred milk in bottles, but when home delivery ceased she had no choice but to switch to supermarket cartons, which she invariably tried to squeeze open at the wrong side, then attacked with a dull paring knife. Like my mother, once she embarked upon a particular course of action, however misguided, she was incapable of reversing it, and the consequences could be explosive, even bloody. Many times I'd found her in the kitchen, emitting a high, throaty moan, with a pool of milk dyed pink at her feet. When I asked what happened, she'd show me her punctured thumb or wrist and say, in the voice of a little girl, "I hurt me," as if the wound itself was the explanation I'd asked for.

In no time her ferocious, irrational attacks on these cartons became legend, the stuff of sidesplitting comedy when reenacted at family gatherings, but as a boy, though I couldn't have articulated why, they troubled me. That someone would remain so faithful to a misbegotten strategy made no sense to me, and like most children I wanted things to make sense, for the world to be a rational place. "Gram," I'd say, picking up the mutilated carton from the floor, "look." And then I'd squeeze at the correct end, which opened obligingly. I imagined I was showing her that the hurt and blood and mess were all unnecessary, but of course I had it exactly wrong. It was the mutilation of the carton and the wounding that were necessary. These satisfied some need I couldn't begin to fathom but that was, in any case, real.

Moreover, while I couldn't have explained this either, my grandmother's syntax, as well as the little-girl cadence she used only when she'd injured herself, creeped me out. She never said *I hurt myself* but rather *I hurt me,* as if *me* and *I* were different people entirely, and the one holding the paring knife had stabbed an innocent bystander. Showing me her angry gashes and puncture wounds, she always seemed to want sympathy and understanding, but these, though I loved her, I was never able to summon. It seemed to me that such irrational behavior needed to change, that warring with the milk cartons was simple lunacy. Perhaps in some remote sector of my kid's brain I'd also linked my otherwise sane grandmother's short-lived but recurring bouts of madness to whatever it was that possessed my mother from time to time. I'd be much older before I began to see the good talkings-to my mother was always giving herself as somehow related to my grandmother's "I hurt me"—both implying a divided or fractured self—but I might have sensed the correlation even then. Nor would the necessary inference have completely escaped me. If my mother was like my grandmother with her cartons, then she'd never truly learn. Like her own mother, she'd just keep hacking away and hurting herself in the process. Which, forty years later, seemed a pretty fair description of how things stood.

Still, did the fact that my mother was more like her mother than she cared to admit mean that I was more like mine than I cared to? Did the fact that I occasionally had more sympathy for and insight into my mother's behavior than, say, my wife, who was justifiably weary of it, suggest that I was like my mother, as she always so confidently claimed, or simply that I'd been observing her longer? The latter, surely. For compelling evidence I needed to look no farther than the book in my hand. I opened *Hotel du Lac* and read the first page:

> From the window all that could be seen was a receding area of grey. It was to be supposed that beyond the grey garden, which seemed to sprout nothing but the stiffish leaves of some unfamiliar plant, lay the vast grey lake, spreading like an anaesthetic towards the invisible further shore, and beyond that, in imagination only, yet verified by the brochure, the peak of the Dent d'Oche, on which snow might already be slightly and silently falling. For it was late September, out of season; the tourists had gone, the rates were reduced, and there were few inducements for visitors in this small town at the water's edge, whose inhabitants, uncommunicative to begin with, were frequently rendered taciturn by the dense cloud that descended for days at a time.

What in the world had possessed me to think my mother would enjoy a book that began like this? "Grey" was used three times in the first two sentences to describe the physical landscape, and my mother's interior landscape was gray already. Her purpose in reading was to flee that grayness into a brighter, more colorful world. She loved for books to take her to exciting new places, and she might well have enjoyed a novel set in a swank Swiss hotel on a lake, but she never would've wanted to go there out of season at reduced rates after all the interesting people had left. I'd taught the novel at Colby the year before, so its narrative details were still fresh in my mind. The protagonist was a middle-aged writer named Edith Hope, who, unlike Anita Brookner, wrote the kind of romance novels my mother might actually have liked to read. At the hotel Edith meets a man named Neville, who makes her an insulting proposal of marriage, not a love match but a union of convenience that will allow each of them societal "cover" as well as romantic freedom. Lest she reject the unflattering offer out of hand, Neville rather cruelly adds that given Edith's age and rather plain appearance (in her cardigan sweaters she resembles Virginia Woolf), she's unlikely to get a better one.

My Colby students, an otherwise pretty savvy bunch, had immediately identified Neville as the novel's villain, ignoring the more subtle, lifelong cruelty Edith had suffered at the hands of her mother and female friends, the very ones who'd packed her off to Switzerland after she fell in love and made a fool of herself back in London. My female students—all in their early twenties—were particularly unwilling to acknowledge the grim possibility that Neville's offer might in fact be the best Edith would ever get, and they were of one voice in proclaiming that she should reject his cynical proposal and wait for love. If their male classmates thought differently, they held their tongues, suggesting just how thorough the cultural training of the late Eighties had been for both genders.

That, I now recalled, was why I'd given the book to my mother in the first place, because she'd gotten her cultural training in an upstate New York mill town four decades earlier, and I was curious to see if she'd twig to what my female students had ignored. The results of this experiment had been both gratifying and dispiriting. My mother hadn't really enjoyed the book and certainly didn't want to read any more Brookner, but just as I suspected the novel's theme of women's cruelty to women had resonated deeply, and her identification with poor Edith Hope, while not wholehearted, had been sufficient to initiate one of her diatribes against her own mother and sister, who had done their level best, she reminded me, to undermine her at every turn and might ultimately have succeeded in destroying her self-confidence if she hadn't escaped Gloversville when she did. The choice Edith had to make didn't particularly interest her. The solution—as my mother saw it—was to return next year, in season, with a better wardrobe, so she'd likely meet a better class of man. She saw Neville as less of a villain than a nonentity.

All of which was, though I hadn't foreseen it, an entirely predictable response. In truth my mother had always been suspicious of women. If there were two lines at the bank or the post office, she'd invariably queue up in the man's, even if the woman's was shorter. The more important the circumstance—to purchase a money order, say, or pay a bill—the more determined she was to wait. If a new window opened and she was asked by a female clerk if she could be of service, my mother would smile and say, "Thank you, but I'll just wait for the man," as if this were perfectly reasonable, as if hers was the well-established and undeniable preference of both genders. Of course in those days the man *was* more likely to be senior, but it wasn't that so much as the fact that my mother always did better dealing with men. She was attractive, and men often fell all over themselves trying to help her out. If she made a mistake in filling out a form, they'd produce a new one and correct the error themselves, where a woman might've sent her away with fine-print instructions.

But it went deeper than that. The whole time I was growing up, I never knew my mother to have a female friend. There was one woman, a coworker at GE, whom she was close to for a time, until they had a falling-out over what my mother claimed was a betrayal—the other woman getting a promotion my mother had assumed would be hers. This was a pattern that would repeat itself again and again over the next several decades. She'd meet a woman her age, usually at a new job, and they'd discover they had interests in common; a tentative friendship would develop, one that seemed destined to evolve into emotional intimacy, but then something bad would happen. Whether it was friction on the job, or that they'd become interested in the same man, things always ended with my mother feeling backstabbed. She must've been as frequently disappointed by men as she was by women, but she treated these as individual, indeed isolated, cases. Often, when she looked back on a failed romantic relationship, she blamed herself, admitting that all the signs had been there and she'd just been too blind, too taken in, to see through his charm, whereas when a woman disappointed her, all women were to blame, and her resolution not to waste her time on female friendships grew much stronger. That was why I was reluctant for her to so easily surrender her friendship with Dot, her Winslow friend. Their camaraderie had lasted quite a while, and I'd begun to wonder if the relationship's longevity might represent a breakthrough.

But perhaps not. As her reaction to *Hotel du Lac* had demonstrated, her distrust of women was deep-seated. While she must have realized that Brookner, at least thematically, was a potential soul mate, that didn't matter. Though she'd understood the novel far better than anyone in my class, she'd disliked it every bit as much, if for the exact opposite reason. Because it had challenged a received feminist truth about female solidarity, my students had concluded that Brookner was lying to them about the world. Whereas my mother disliked the book precisely because she was being told the truth. That wasn't what she read fiction for.

Indeed, the books I'd spent the afternoon packing—so varied in genre, including historical romances, detective novels, romantic thrillers, travel books—had in common a reassuring conventionality that couldn't entirely be accounted for by the decades, the Thirties through the early Sixties, during which most of them had been written. My mother's large collection of murder mysteries was particularly instructive. She much preferred the English variety, with its emphasis on the restoration of order. In books by her favorite "Golden Age" British mystery writers—Josephine Tey, Margery Allingham, Dorothy Sayers, Ngaio Marsh, John Dickson Carr, and Agatha Christie—evil might lurk around every foggy corner, and murder most foul would throw everything into temporary flux, but in the end the detective, often a rogue aristocrat like Lord Peter Wimsey or Roderick Alleyn, ferreted out the culprit in a stunning display of logic, intuition and, often, an understanding of complex social realities for which aristocrats, in novels like these if nowhere else, are famous.

American murder mysteries left her cold. She thought they were less clever, which was true enough; Raymond Chandler famously couldn't follow his own plots. But they also operated on an entirely different set of premises. Here detectives didn't solve crimes by means of brilliant deductions or arcane knowledge. In American detective novels the hero's primary virtues are his honesty and his ability to take a punch. Sam Spade hasn't much interest in restoring order because, as he knows all too well, that order was corrupt to begin with. Villains are typically either rich men who made their money dishonestly or, worse yet, people of limited moral imagination who aspire only to what money and power can buy, who want to move up in class and don't care how. In this noir world, cops are on the take, lawyers and judges all have a price, as do doctors and newspapermen. In a sea of corruption your only hope is a lone man, someone *you* can hire but who can't be bought off by anybody who has more money. There probably is no figure in literature more romantic than Philip Marlowe, whose very name suggests knight-errantry, and my mother was herself a romantic of the first order, but she had no more use for Marlowe than she had for Anita Brookner. Men like Marlowe always ended up telling her what she didn't want to hear. Okay, he might find your missing child or husband, but often you'd end up wishing he hadn't, because he'd also find out something you didn't want to know about that child or husband or even yourself, something you'd been trying hard not to look at, or admit to. What kind of escape was that? Better to get good news from a fop like Lord Peter, whose sell-by date in the real world would have long since expired, had anyone like him ever existed in the first place.

The historical novels my mother favored were similarly revealing. They featured a brave, stalwart heroine who invariably would prove herself worthy of the dashing fellow she'd fallen in love with, often by testing her mettle in his world. If she fell in love with a pirate, she might for a time become a pirate herself. Their freedom from social mores, however, was understood to be a phase, like adolescence, and their adventures always culminated in marriage, an institution that would tame the heroine's wilder impulses and make the hero a responsible citizen. To facilitate these matters, the former rogue would be discovered to be actually an aristocrat who'd been cheated out of his estate, which in the final chapter is restored to him. It was a complicated fantasy, one that allowed my mother to think of herself as a rebel while actually being, in her heart of hearts, a conformist. Though she claimed not to be a prude, she preferred sex not to be explicit but rather relegated to the space breaks or implied by the coy nicknames ("my sugar wench") given the heroine by her paramour. Reality, especially of the grim sort, should at all costs be kept at bay, regardless of the genre. She claimed to love anything about Ireland or England or Spain, but in fact she needed books in these settings to be warm and comfy, more like Maeve Binchy than William Trevor. Not surprisingly, given that she'd felt trapped most of her life, she loved books about time travel, but only if the places the characters traveled to were ones she was interested in. She had exactly no interest in the future or in any past that didn't involve romantic adventure.

Still, illuminating though literary taste can be, the more I thought about it, neither my mother's library nor my own meant quite what I wanted it to. If my books were more serious and literary than hers, that was due more to nurture than nature. If I didn't read much escapist fiction, it was because I lived a blessed life from which I neither needed nor desired to escape. I wasn't a superior person, just an educated one, and for that in large measure I had my mother to thank. Maybe she'd tried to talk me out of becoming a writer, but she was more responsible than anyone for my being one. Back when we lived on Helwig Street, at the end of her long workdays at GE, after making her scant supper and cleaning up, after doing the laundry (without benefit of a washing machine) and ironing, after making sure

I was set for school the next day, she might've collapsed in front of the television, but she didn't. She read. Every night. Her taste, unformed as mine would later be by a score of literature professors, was equally dogmatic; she read her Daphne du Mauriers and Mary Stewarts until their covers fell off and had to be replaced. It was from my mother that I learned reading was not a duty but a reward, and from her that I intuited a vital truth: most people are trapped in a solitary existence, a life circumscribed by want and failures of imagination, limitations from which readers are exempt. You can't make a writer without first making a reader, and that's what my mother made me. Moreover, though I'd outgrown her books, they had a hand in shaping the kind of writer I'd eventually become—one who, unlike many university-trained writers, didn't consider *plot* a dirty word, who paid attention to audience and pacing, who had little tolerance for literary pretension.

No, in order to make the case that my mother and I weren't two peas in a genetic pod, I needed to identify something in my basic nature, some habit of mind or innate ability that I'd always possessed, traceable all the way back to who I'd been on Helwig Street, not who I'd become in the meantime. Was it possible I was literally staring at it? Could it be that our bookshelves—not the books themselves or what was in them but rather their current haphazard arrangement—provided the answer to why my mother and I were forever at loggerheads? Two weeks earlier, Barbara and I had hastily thrown onto the shelves as many books as would fit, then moved on to more pressing tasks. Indeed, since moving to Camden, we'd been in what I thought of as "this now, that later" mode. With dozens of tasks to complete each day (with everything, to borrow my mother's word, *unsettled*), they all were constantly being prioritized and reprioritized. *This now, that later* mode was all about making sound decisions on the fly about what had to be attended to now and what could wait. Logic and reason were important, but often you had to go on intuition and feel. What you saw in your peripheral vision could be as important as what you were looking at directly. On the basis of incomplete data, you had to make educated guesses and try to see three or four moves in advance, to anticipate the Law of Unintended Consequences before it kicked in. Just as vital, you had to accept that you were going to make mistakes from time to time. When you messed up, it was important not to mind and even more important to promptly reverse course. You also had to understand that at any given moment there were decisions you simply couldn't make yet and have faith that given time some problems would resolve themselves. What we were engaged in was a kind of domestic triage, and I'd always been pretty good at that, God only knew why, because this was something completely left out of my mother. I hadn't forgotten how, back in Phoenix, I'd had to reorder her daily to-do lists so they made at least a little sense and we didn't waste time retracing our steps. At eighteen I was already cringing at her due-south instincts and her inability, once she'd begun a task, to abandon it for a more important one. She couldn't possibly have lived with the chaos of our bookshelves for two days, much less two weeks. Even as a young man I could see how much her faulty decision making was costing her, that because of her inflexible adherence to poor sequencing she was forever discovering, too late, that her ship, which could easily have been turned around while out at sea, now had to be rotated in the cramped harbor.

It now occurred to me that I'd been trying to resequence my mother's to-do lists ever since, with decidedly mixed results. Sometimes she'd grasp my organizing principle and say, "Oh, aren't you clever!" But more often she'd insist on doing things her own way and become monumentally annoyed when I pointed out that B really had to follow A, that getting A right was the key to both B and C, that A was the necessary foundation upon which the remaining alphabet would rest. To this she'd respond that different people saw things differently, and that to her, B was more important than A. Worse, she was always so proud of her tortured logic. She loved to explicate, detail by wobbly detail, how she'd arrived at her dubious conclusions. She wasn't unlike the detectives in her locked-room mysteries, who would reveal in the final excruciating chapter how the villainous deed was done, that the murderer was legless, which was why, once he'd removed his prostheses, no one had observed him running away on his stumps on the far side of the shoulder-high hedge. Leaving the reader to say, "I'm sorry, *what*?"

When I was eighteen and my mother in her forties, our disagreements over process were seldom serious. She liked to say there was more than one way to skin a cat and that when I got to be her age I'd have odd habits, too. But over the years, as I became increasingly responsible for the outcomes of her insistence on doing things out of their natural and practical order, together with my growing impatience with her interminable, brain-scalding explanations, there were more serious disputes. At times, rather than argue, I'd just throw up my hands. "Do what you want," I'd tell her, halfway out the door. "Let me know how it turns out." And sometimes, the phone would ring an hour later, and she'd say, "*Now* I see what you meant." But just as often her voice would be triumphant, once she'd somehow succeeded in forcing the square peg into the round hole with a mallet and now was eager to explain the brilliance of her violent solution. This, then, was surely what I was looking for: the hardwired difference, probably genetic in origin, between my mother and me, the root of our ongoing conflict and the reason that I was seldom able, as she put it, "to take her side."

Except this didn't really wash either. For one thing, while it might be true that I was good at domestic triage and she sucked at it, a more significant truth was that my mother and grandmother weren't the only ones who wouldn't stop flying in the face of reason. It would've been nice to see myself as Sisyphus and my current exhaustion as existential, the result of three-plus decades of attempting to correctly sequence my mother's metaphorical to-do lists without her permission or assistance. But in fact I was worn out from dealing with the consequences of what I myself had set in motion back in the spring when I stubbornly ignored Barbara's *or*. Because surely some part of me had known it was folly to plant that FOR SALE sign in front of our Waterville home and even worse folly to imagine I could put my mother and her needs on the back burner for however long it took for us to get settled.

More specifically, the time had come to admit that none of my plan was working out. Since moving to Camden, we'd become a literally divided family. The girls' bedrooms were on the second floor of the main house; Barb and I occupied the apartment over the garage, so we were often not aware of their comings and goings. We'd planned on using money from the sale of the Waterville property to convert the upstairs apartment into our master bedroom suite, but it hadn't even been shown in more than a month, which meant we might be exiled from our house-in-progress for the foreseeable future while carrying *two* mortgages. In another six weeks Emily's college tuition would come due, as would Kate's to her new prep school. The upscale assisted-living apartment we'd eventually found for my mother would cost almost as much as a third tuition. We were keeping the rent a secret from her, but she was bound to find out soon. Barbara, having quit her job at Colby, was looking for work on the coast and not finding any, and my West Coast film agent was looking for screen projects for me and not finding any, and at long last it was becoming clear that the back-end money I'd been hoping for from the *Nobody's Fool* movie wasn't going to materialize for the simple reason that there wasn't any, at least not for writers, and only a fool would have believed otherwise. As if all this weren't enough, I was still a good year from delivering (and getting paid for) my next novel. The problem wasn't sequencing but rather my unwillingness to admit I'd been wrong. After realizing how the Camden house could be made to work for us and then imagining us in it, I'd become not only determined to see it through but also blind to reason. While there'd been numerous opportunities to turn this ship around, I'd stubbornly held to our dubious course, expertly navigating us into Camden's tiny, expensive harbor, where we were now trapped.

All of which was beginning to feel like a cosmic I-told-you-so. My mother's deep conviction had always been that she and I were cut from the same cloth. From the time I was a boy, whenever we disagreed, she'd tell me that later on, when I was her age, I'd think as she did, an assertion that never failed to infuriate me, suggesting as it did that I wasn't her offspring but her clone, and over the years nothing gave me more pleasure than to reflect on how wrong she was, that I most assuredly didn't think like she did, and that time had only widened this gap, not narrowed it. What I hadn't realized was that in addition to being dead wrong, she was also profoundly right, or would have been if her claim had been articulated just a little differently. She said I'd one day *think* as she did; what she probably meant was that one day I'd *be* like her—obsessive, dogged, and rigid.

How could I have failed to see in myself the very traits I'd so confidently assigned to her? The evidence was everywhere. Take, for instance, my freshman year at the university, when I'd become addicted to, of all things, pinball. For several months a particular machine in the basement of the student center took total possession of my mind. It had begun innocently enough. One evening, after dinner at the cafeteria, I'd visited the game room with some friends and wasted a couple of quarters, which back then got you three plays. The next night, though, I'd returned without my friends, and the night after that. Very quickly I began thinking of this machine as mine and during dinner would become panicky at the thought of somebody getting on it before I could. Once I'd claimed the machine, if I had a run of bad luck that necessitated my leaving it to get more quarters, and some other sallow, pathetic nerd was at its controls when I returned, I'd have to swallow a black, homicidal fury. In a matter of days there was simply no life outside the game room. I went to class, of course, but even there, as my professors spoke, I could hear my machine's distinctive clangs and clanks on the other side of campus, its score hurtling upward, registering bonus points from the bumpers and targets that were hardest to hit, then the lovely, sweet thunk of free games popping up in its tiny window, a sound that caused the other wretched denizens of the game room to suspend their own activities and crowd around. Soon, to ensure I'd have enough quarters to play for a couple of hours, I started selling my evening meal ticket, telling myself I wasn't hungry anyway, and playing late into the evening when I should have been studying, stopping only when my luck and skill ran out. Worse, since I always told my roommates I was going to the library, they regarded my late nights and my pale, drained appearance when I finally returned to the dorm as evidence of a virtuous dedication they themselves lacked. There were girls from my classes I wanted to ask out, but whatever money I set aside for the weekend would be gone by midweek. I lost weight, becoming as wraithlike as Gollum with his "Precious." For months that inexplicable and humiliating madness held me in its grip until one evening, on my very first quarter, I entered some kind of zone, winning so many free games that the thought of actually playing them made me ill. Suddenly both sated and sane, I simply walked away and never went back.

A couple years later, though, in graduate school, I was seized by my father's particular mania and found myself on a shuttle between the grungy dog track in South Tucson and any nickel-and-dime poker table I could find. The track was particularly depressing, a magnet for the city's poorest and most desperate souls. Friday nights were the worst because you could tell at a glance that some of the men had come directly from work, that instead of going home, they'd cashed their paychecks at the track and were betting the week's grocery money. I recognized them—the way they studied the racing form so furtively, their darting eyes mining the abstruse data for tips; they were Gloversville men, somehow magically transported to the desert, and here I was among them again. Being a literature student, I was of course susceptible to metaphor, and when the mechanical rabbit made the turn in front of the starting gate and the foolish greyhounds bolted after it, I remember wondering if I was the only one in the park who understood its terrible significance, and if that made me any smarter or dumber than these guys with low-wage, dead-end jobs. Poker? Well, betting nickels, dimes, and quarters you couldn't get hurt too bad. That's what I told myself, but you be the judge.

Even more horrifying than such ugly, stupid obsessions

was the fact that I couldn't even take credit for triumphing over them. The day I sold blood to buy my way into a poker game, I hadn't looked at myself in the mirror and said, *Enough.* Nor, to borrow my mother's phrase, had I given myself a good talking-to. That would have been pointless. I knew myself well enough to know I wasn't listening. No, I'd simply bided my time and waited for the current madness to run its course, after which it would likely be replaced by some new, as-yet-unimagined idiocy, no doubt every bit as humiliating and self-destructive as the last. Or perhaps worse. This was what really terrified me. If I could be seduced by a pinball machine, by the tacky allure of a dog track, what would I do if I was offered a real temptation? What if my next obsession took the form of a woman? Would I give myself a good talking-to then, reminding myself that I loved my wife, that I'd been preparing for a life of the mind, that I wanted to be a good man? Or would I become a character out of a Jim Thompson novel, pathetic and helpless in the grip of something strong and merciless and utterly relentless? It was possible.

The Camden house was empty and still. My daughters had taken summer jobs at a popular waterfront restaurant, and Barbara was off somewhere. I'd been looking forward to seeing them when I got home, a distraction from the guilt and fear and dread that had gnawed at me as I'd driven home from Winslow, to our chaotic, jumbled library, with its boxes waiting to be unpacked. But for some reason I now felt like unfit company and was grateful to be alone. Unless I was mistaken, something inside my mother had finally broken, and it was my fault. I thought about calling her and apologizing for every-thing, especially for asking her to do something I knew she was incapable of: to be patient for an unspecified period of time, to live with every last thing up in the air. But then I remembered that she was going out to dinner with Dot.

Across the room, on a high shelf, were copies of books I'd written and literary periodicals where I'd published stories and essays and reviews. Rising at last, I walked over and ran my fingers along their spines, smiling not so much with pleasure at the achievement as with the realization of its source. The big-gest difference between my mother and me, I now saw clearly, had less to do with either nature or nurture than with blind dumb luck, the third and often lethal rail of human destiny. My next obsession might well have been a woman, or a narcotic, or a bottle of tequila. Instead I'd stumbled on storytelling and become infected. Halfway through my doctoral dissertation, I'd nearly quit so I could write full-time. Not because I imag-ined I was particularly gifted or that one day I'd be able to earn a living. I simply had to. It was the game room and the dog track all over again. An unreasoning fit of *must*. That, no doubt, was what my mother had recognized and abhorred, what had caused her to remind me about my responsibilities as a husband and father.

It didn't take long for me to learn that novel writing was a line of work that suited my temperament and played to my strengths, such as they were. Because—and don't let anybody tell you different—novel writing is mostly triage (*this now, that later*) and obstinacy. Feeling your way around in the dark, trying to anticipate the Law of Unintended Consequences. Living with and welcoming uncertainty. Trying something, and when that doesn't work, trying something else. Welcoming clutter. Surrendering a good idea for a better one. Knowing you won't find the finish line for a year or two, or five, or maybe never, without caring much. Putting one foot in front of the other. Taking small bites, chewing thoroughly. Grinding it out. Knowing that when you've finally settled everything that can be, you'll immediately seek out more chaos. Rinse and repeat. Somehow, without ever intending to, I'd discovered how to turn obsession and what my grandmother used to call sheer cussedness—character traits that had dogged both my parents, causing them no end of difficulty—to my advantage. The same qualities that over a lifetime had contracted my mother's world had somehow expanded mine. How and by what mechanism? Dumb luck? Grace? I honestly have no idea. Call it whatever you want—except virtue.

Real Time

WHEN SHE OPENED the door, I took an involuntary step back at the sight. Her hair wild, her eyes wide and frantic, she was still in her nightgown, the madwoman in the attic, straight out of *Jane Eyre*. She grabbed my arm, pulling me inside. "What time is it?"

Eight forty-five, I told her. I'd arrived, as I always did, at the appointed moment. Being late, even by a minute or two, was always a mistake. When I knocked, she'd often open the door before my hand could fall to my side; in winter she'd already have her coat on, her purse over her arm. "I saw you from the kitchen window when you pulled in," she'd say, as if waiting at the window was less nutty than waiting at the door. So what on earth was this? Had she overslept? Given how lethargic she'd been lately, it was possible.

But she wasn't lethargic now. Indeed, when I told her the

time, she flew across the room with alarming haste, especially given her claim that her legs always locked up whenever she had to hurry. On the pad of paper she kept next to her telephone, she scrawled *8:45* and, underneath that, *REAL TIME*. Then she stared at the pad, as if expecting the words or numbers to change before her eyes.

"Mom," I said. "Why did you write down the time?"

"So I'll know," she said, still studying what she'd just scribbled.

"Know what?"

"The time. Later, I'll want to know."

"But it won't be eight forty-five anymore."

When she stared at me blankly, I decided to try a different tack. "Mom, did you forget about the doctor?" We were due at his office in half an hour.

Abject terror now. "Did we miss the appointment?"

"No, there's plenty of time. But you need to get dressed."

"I can't."

"Why not?"

"I haven't showered. I didn't know what time it was."

"You can shower when you get home."

She blinked at me in incomprehension, then gazed aimlessly around her new apartment. Was *this* home?

"Do you think you can get dressed?" She followed me into the bedroom, where the clothes she'd planned to wear were hanging on the inside doorknob. I pointed out her dresser, where the day before she and Barbara had arranged her undergarments in the top drawers.

She sat down on the bed. "I need to think." She picked up her alarm clock and peered at it. For some reason it said 3:17.

"You need to get dressed, Mom. So we can go to the doctor."

Terror again. "Did we miss the appointment?"

"Just get dressed, okay?"

In the living room I called home, catching Barbara just as she was about to leave the house to run an errand. "I need you," I told her. "Right away, actually."

"What's wrong?"

"I wish I knew. Maybe another TIA." Somehow I didn't think so, though. Her ministrokes always left my mother exhausted, one side of her face tingling, her speech for a time impaired. But she always knew what they were and what had just happened to her. This was something new. Except for the fact that she wasn't making any sense, her speech seemed fine. "She's disoriented. Confused."

It would take Barbara twenty minutes to get here. I called the doctor's office to say we'd be a few minutes late. Setting the receiver back in its cradle, I noticed that the clock on the lamp table said 11:22. The one on top of the TV said 7:03; the one on the stove, 1:54. All these clocks had been set correctly the day before. "How you coming, Mom?" I called.

No answer.

The bedroom door was open. "Mom?" I said.

She was sitting on the bed, still in her nightgown, her back to me. Morning light was filtering in through the curtain, but the room was dark. In her hands was her favorite clock, the gold-plated one I'd bought her for Christmas years ago. At first I thought she was winding it, and started to tell her that while time was of the essence, the clock, ironically, wasn't. She wasn't winding it, though, just making the hands go around, minutes and then whole hours, passing in a few seconds.

I sat down next to her. "Mom," I said. "What's wrong? Can you tell me?"

"Why do the hands go this way?" she said.

When it was clear I didn't understand, she made the universal motion indicating clockwise. What she wanted me to explain was why the hands wouldn't go in the opposite direction. Still anxious that I understand, she demonstrated by twisting the stem counterclockwise, grunting with the effort.

"You're going to break it," I told her. "See, you've already bent the stem."

This didn't interest her. The mystery she was trying to fathom ran much deeper than that.

AMAZINGLY, EVERYTHING HAD gone off without a hitch. The movers had arrived in Winslow when they were supposed to and immediately went to work. I fully expected my mother to renege on our agreement and demand to stay behind and ramrod the whole job, but instead she got in the car with Barbara and off they went to Camden, leaving me to inventory her possessions as they were carried out the door. "This lady moves a lot," one of the men remarked. He had her dinette upside down on the floor (which, had my mother been there, would have elicited cries of *Oooh! Oooh! You're scratching it!*) and was unscrewing its legs. The table's underside sported several stickers in different colors applied from previous moves.

At one point Dot stopped by, and I learned they hadn't gone out to dinner after all, that my mother had phoned to say she was too tired. "I've never seen anybody so worked up," Dot said.

"It's like this with every move," I told her.

"I don't know if it's the move or the idea of a new doctor," Dot said.

Which was true, of course. Changing doctors always weighed heavily on my mother, because she had a good dozen prescriptions that would need to be filled; high on her list of anxieties was whether the new drugstore and the new doctor communicated effectively, otherwise giving her the wrong meds or leaving her totally without. A new doctor also meant unwelcome questions, about her unhealthy eating habits and lack of exercise and all manner of things she considered nobody else's business. It had taken her a long time, but she'd managed to train her Waterville doctor to accept what she told him as true and to write the scripts she believed she needed, including, for the past few years, Paxil, about which I was beginning to hear disturbing stories. The new doctor might express misgivings about the efficacy of all this.

"She says she's exhausted from having so much to do," Dot continued, "but when I ask her what I can help with, there doesn't seem to be anything."

"You can't help her worry."

"I also said I hoped we'd be able to keep in touch. Camden's not so far, but I got the impression she's not interested."

"Maybe after she's settled," I said hopefully, though I was pretty sure their friendship was over. My mother hated all maybes, ifs, and whens, preferring to resolve things badly than leave them up in the air with a good outcome a mere possibility. "Thanks for being such a good friend."

"I'll miss her," Dot said. Then she added, almost apologetically, "I really like your mom, it's just a shame she's so . . ." She struggled to find the right word but finally gave up. Either that or the word *impossible* suggested itself, and she was too kind to use it. "Maybe that's why I like her. Being your own worst enemy is something I understand."

Later, back on the coast and armed with my diagram of the new apartment, I told the movers where to put the furniture and stack the boxes of books. "Wow," said the guy who'd mentioned how often my mother moved, taking the place in. "I wouldn't mind living here myself."

I stifled the urge to tell him to check back in a few months when this very apartment would probably be available. Because my mother was clearly going to hate it here. We'd looked everywhere, coming up against the exact same obstacles that had plagued us inland. She preferred not to live among old people, because all they ever talked about was their illnesses and their new meds and which of their daughters was ignoring them this week and which would be visiting next. She wanted someplace lively, like where she'd first lived in Phoenix. She wanted to feel alive, and for that you needed young people. With young people, however, came music and noise and children, and she wanted none of that. She couldn't have anyone living overhead. Underfoot would be okay, except that she couldn't manage stairs, which pretty much ruled that out. She preferred apartment complexes but hated subsidized places, because the law didn't allow them to discriminate, and you might end up living next door to some Section 8 nutjob. Unsubsidized places she couldn't afford, and she didn't want us making up the difference, especially if it was considerable. And we knew from experience that whatever she settled on had to be within half an hour from Camden. Nothing we'd seen was suitable and, to complete the Woody Allen joke, they all had long waiting lists.

The place I thought would be best for her, Megunticook House, was actually in Camden. The rents were subsidized, and she clearly qualified. The residents were all elderly, and the complex provided no services, so by and large they weren't terribly infirm. The apartments themselves were nice, the grounds clean and neat, but when we pulled in she took one look and said, "Oh, Rick . . . really, I don't think so, do you?"

"Could we look, at least?"

She grudgingly agreed, but it was clearly a no-go. "Shabby," she explained later, when we were back in the car. "Did you see how run-down the whole place was? And did you see all the walkers there in the foyer? People who need those should keep them in their rooms. Didn't you notice how the paint was peeling outside?"

I explained that we were now on the coast and the complex

was a quarter mile from the ocean, with harsh winters and salt air, well, paint peeled.

"I couldn't live there," she said. "The other place was better."

By this she meant Woodland Hills, an assisted-living facility in Rockland, twenty minutes away. Its long drive and carefully manicured grounds made it resemble a country club, but this, too, had put her off. "I don't need anything *this* posh," she said. Inside, the corridors were wide enough that two wheelchairs could pass each other going in opposite directions, and handrails were affixed to all the walls. There were endless activities—from wheelchair aerobics to computer classes—and she wasn't interested in any of them. "I'm used to living independently," she explained to the lady who showed us around. She naturally didn't care about the van that took residents to the supermarket and doctors' offices: "My son does all that." The meals were served in a large dining room, though the schedule instantly offended her. "Who eats their main meal at noon?" she said once we were back in the car.

"Well . . . ," I began.

"Assisted living, my foot," she said. "That's a nursing home. There wasn't anyone there who walked without a cane."

"The apartment itself was nice," I pointed out for the sake of argument. "Light and airy." Better yet, she'd run her index finger over the surface of the stove, and I could tell it had come away clean. "Plus there's no waiting list."

"Let's keep looking," she said.

And so we had, until there was nothing left to look at.

———

MARK, MY MOTHER'S NEW DOCTOR, was less than half her age. Having recently taken on Barbara and me and the girls, he'd agreed to see her as well. He was new in town but already had a reputation as an excellent diagnostician. His manner was no nonsense to the point of being brusque, so I was surprised when he tenderly took my mother's hand. "Okay, Jean," he said, "I'm going to give you four words and ask you to remember them. Then we're going to chat for a while, and then I'm going to ask you to tell me what the four words were. Do you understand?"

My mother nodded, before glancing over at me for confirmation, as if her understanding were an issue I could speak to.

"Here are the four words: *bird, window, car, book.*"

Good, I thought. She'll get *book,* at least.

Barbara had somehow managed to get her dressed, and we'd only been half an hour late. I'd quietly informed the admitting nurse of the basics, that this was supposed to be a get-acquainted appointment but that my mother had been disoriented when I arrived to pick her up, that for some reason she was obsessing about clocks and time, and that I'd never seen her like this before. We were now—Barbara and the doctor and my mother and me—in one of his small consulting rooms.

"How are you feeling today?" the doctor asked her.

She turned to me. "What time is it?"

I told her (three minutes later than the last time she asked, just before we left the waiting room).

"Jean. Can you look at me?"

Good, I thought again. A strong male voice. She responds well to those. My own the obvious exception.

"How are you feeling?"

"I'm a little worried," she confessed.

"About what?"

"The time."

"Why are you worried about the time?"

"I have a very important doctor's appointment."

"You're at your appointment now. I'm your doctor. You don't have to worry about that anymore, okay?"

My mother looked greatly relieved to learn it and smiled over at me.

"Do you know what time of year it is?"

She thought about it, then admitted she wasn't sure.

"Can you tell me where you live?"

She again looked over at me. "Woodland Hills," I told him, immediately flushing, because of course he didn't care where she lived. He just wanted to know if she knew. "She just moved in," I explained.

"And who's the president?"

She smiled. Here was an answer she knew. She started to answer, then suddenly couldn't remember. She turned to me. After all, I'd supplied the last answer, so maybe I knew this, too. "Oh," she said, nudging me, "*you* know."

I tried to send her a telepathic message. *George W. Bush. You hate the little twerp. You're hoping to live long enough to see him indicted for crimes against humanity. Remember?*

But she didn't. She remembered neither the man nor how much she loathed him. My heart sank then, because the look on her face suggested in addition to being stumped by the question, she was beginning to grasp that something was terribly wrong. Or maybe she was just mimicking the look on my own face.

"How about those words?" the doctor asked. "Can you tell me what the four words were?"

My mother shook her head and then let it hang, completely out of answers.

WHEN HE FINISHED his examination, Mark took me aside. "Your mother is suffering from dementia," he said.

I nodded, not terribly surprised, given what had transpired in the consulting room. Still, something seemed wrong. "But why?"

"We don't know the cause, exactly, but it's not unusual in people your mother's age."

"Yeah," I said, "but overnight?"

"The onset of symptoms can appear rapid."

Something about his use of *appear* made me wonder if we were talking at cross-purposes. "Yesterday, she was fine."

At this he knitted his brow, clearly dubious.

"She's been very anxious about the move. She's been having TIAs over the last couple years. Is it possible she had one during the night?"

"Where was she living before Woodland Hills?"

"She had an apartment in Winslow."

He looked like I'd just given him a stiff left jab. "An apartment."

"Yes."

"Are you telling me that your mother's been living alone?"

"Yes. The only reason she's in Woodland is that they had a vacancy."

"Yesterday she could have remembered all four words? She'd have known who the president was?"

"Absolutely. She'd have shared her opinion of him, which is low. And she certainly wouldn't have forgotten the word *book*." When he still appeared doubtful, I added, "She's been living independently," realizing as soon as I said it that she would've been thrilled by this representation.

"She isn't normally confused?"

This question was more difficult. "She likes to rearrange facts," I admitted. "She prefers her own version of things. But nothing like what you saw in there."

"Tell me about her medications."

I did, at least the ones I could remember—for high blood pressure, the thyroid, the anxiety, the acid reflux, the arthritis, a couple other things.

"Let me do some research," he told me. "If she's been upset about the move, it's possible the veil will lift. Can you bring her home with you for a few days?"

I thought of Barbara, who'd bear the brunt of this—the dressing and undressing and bathing. And I thought of what it would look like if I said no.

Noting my reluctance, he said, "She really shouldn't be left alone in this condition."

"Of course not," I said as we emerged into the outer office, where Barbara and my mother were waiting. My wife had heard the last part, and our eyes met. "I'm just not sure we can handle her."

"It doesn't look like she'll be much trouble," he said, and I really couldn't blame him for not understanding. My mother had been docile as a lamb during the examination, and she weighed all of ninety pounds. What the hell kind of son would hesitate to take his *mother,* a sick and confused and lost old woman, into his home for a few days? Of course, I wasn't worried about my mother in her present condition, but of what might occur if, as he put it, the veil lifted.

"How about you bring her back tomorrow," he suggested, "and we'll see how things are progressing?"

I took a deep breath. "Okay," I said. "Sure."

ON THE RIDE BACK to Camden she continued to ask what time it was every few minutes, apparently still worried about missing the doctor's appointment that was now safely consigned to the past. At home we installed her in the guest room with all the books, but nothing in the real, physical world seemed to interest her but the gold-plated clock, which she refused to set down. She continued to spin the hands round and around, as if she feared time itself would stop if she quit.

Hoping to distract her, we turned on the TV in the family room and found an old movie we thought might interest her. It was only a matter of, well, time before she broke her clock, so I suggested we put it on top of the television where she could see it from the sofa. She reluctantly agreed, but then sat there staring at it as if the movie weren't playing. Every time I got up to answer the phone or get something from the kitchen, she'd have the clock in her lap again by the time I returned, still fast-forwarding its hands. Emily, our older daughter, was working the lunch shift and missing all this, but at one point I went into the living room and found her sister, Kate, sobbing in front of the fireplace. "It's just so terrible" was all she could say. Midafternoon, Emily called to say she'd been asked to stay on for the evening shift as well, and I encouraged her to. After all, there was nothing she could do, and seeing her grandmother in her present state would have torn her up. Kate went to work that evening herself, which left Barbara and me alone with my mother, whose interest continued to be strictly chronographic.

Instead of lifting, the veil that had lowered over her rationality seemed to descend even further. As the hours passed she became increasingly anxious, though she couldn't explain why. We tried to get her to eat something, but that would have involved putting down her clock. By early evening it was becoming apparent that bringing her home had been a mistake. I called the doctor's office, which by then was closed, and left a message with Mark's service. When he returned the call half an hour later, I described our dilemma. Far from calming down, my mother was becoming more and more agitated. She was still obsessing about time and trying to understand how it worked and how to make it stay put or, better yet, reverse course. What worried us the most was what might happen that night. Barbara and I couldn't sleep in our apartment over the garage—that was too far away. We'd either have to take turns outside her bedroom door or risk finding my mother out walking the streets of Camden in her nightgown. This last fear seemed to convince him. "Do you think you can get her to come to the emergency room?"

Normally, getting my mother to do anything she was disinclined to would have been a struggle, but not now. I'd simply ask to see her clock, then tell her I'd give it back to her as soon as we were in the car. She'd follow that clock anywhere.

"THE *FIRST* THING I'm going to do," my mother announced from the backseat, "is get a new doctor."

We weren't even out of the hospital parking lot when she dropped this bombshell. Clearly she'd been saving it for some time and was anxious to see just how large a crater its impact would create. After four days in the hospital things had returned to the old normal, her new obsession and recent lethargy now past. Concerned about the number of medications she was taking and their possible negative interactions, and needing to establish some sort of baseline, Mark took her off everything but her blood pressure pills. When her blood work came back, it revealed a massive sodium imbalance, caused in large part by the heavily salted, overly processed frozen foods that represented her entire diet. It was also possible that her worries about moving yet again had gotten the upper hand, and she'd been overmedicating. At any rate, within hours her rationality began to return—along with a tremendous fury. For the hospital staff it was unnerving to see an almost-eighty-year-old woman "wake up" from her sleepy doldrums so monumentally pissed off.

For my mother, of course, being rational didn't guarantee that she'd now arrive at valid conclusions. *"Bird, window, car, book,"* she continued. "Does he think I'm crazy? That I can't remember four simple words?"

Before releasing her from the hospital, Mark had given her the same examination that had been such a disaster earlier, including the memory test, and this time she'd rattled off the four words effortlessly. I was impressed, since on neither occasion had I been able to recall them all myself. She'd also given him her thoughts on Bush, which seemed to please him, though perhaps he was merely heartened by her lucidity.

Barbara was at the wheel, so I could turn around to look at my mother. "The last time he asked you about those same four words, you couldn't recall even one," I told her, not without misgiving. She had little memory of the days leading up to her hospitalization, and I knew this troubled her greatly. As her world had begun shrinking over the last decade, her need to control whatever remained became paramount, and the idea of losing time, of having to ask for help to fill in the blanks, left her both frightened and unmoored. She'd grilled both her granddaughters about the event she couldn't remember, as if Emily and Kate could be trusted more than their parents, who for all she knew might be in league with the doctor she now pledged to shitcan.

"You've been very sick."

"And who does he think he is, saying I can't have my Paxil?" she continued, impossible, as always, to corner when she'd built up a head of steam and was determined to let it off.

"He thinks he's your doctor."

"Then I'll call my old doctor. He'll prescribe it."

"Actually, no, Mom, he won't."

"Plus," she noted, "I've got a good two-month supply at home."

At this Barbara and I exchanged glances. One of our first duties after she was admitted to the hospital had been to gather all her meds from the Woodland Hills apartment and bring them in. The stash she was counting on was gone, and I felt like a parent who'd disposed of the weed he discovered in the back of his kid's closet.

My mother's real beef with Mark was his quiet, calm refusal to be bamboozled. It was as if he wasn't treating *my* mother but his own. He was onto all of her tricks in a heartbeat. When she evaded his questions, he simply repeated them. When she pointed this out to him, he assured her that as soon as she gave him a clear, honest answer he'd be happy to move on to a new topic.

"Telling me what I can and can't eat," she continued, "like I'm a child."

"I'm sorry you aren't fond of him, but he's a good doctor, and he did save your life."

"Piffle," she said, but then she fell silent, examining the ugly blood blister on her right thumb that had resulted from her twisting the stem of that damn clock for hours on end. Was she considering the larger implications of harming herself without meaning to? Her bedrock conviction in life had always been: *I know what's best for me.* Had enough evidence to the contrary finally caused her to reconsider? Might she be entering a new phase of trusting the wisdom of others and doubting her own? Was it possible at eighty to shift gears so fundamentally?

"How long will I be staying with you, then?" she wanted to know.

"As long as you need to." We'd been over this before, of course. She was in withdrawal, and the next few days were bound to be so ugly that she'd need companionship and support to survive them.

"Is there a lot to do at the apartment?"

"Very little," I assured her, which was true. I told her again how, in addition to Barb and me, the girls had pitched in to get everything ready for her, the clothes hung up in the closet, her dishes and glasses in the cupboards. She'd told us where she wanted things, and we'd followed these instructions she now couldn't remember giving. The aluminum foil and plastic wrap and wax paper rolls were safe in the oven, an appliance she had no other use for, relying on the microwave to warm her frozen dinners. She and Barbara had already arranged her bedroom, and we'd hung her pictures and mirrors on the walls. The television was hooked up, the cable turned on, the phone service activated. She and I would need to go grocery shopping soon, and she'd no doubt want to make a few cosmetic changes, but otherwise she was good to go. "And of course we'll have to reset all the clocks," I added.

For her, that had been the scariest detail of all. In the hospital, after the fog had lifted, I told her about how we sat on the edge of the bed the morning of her first doctor's appointment and she asked why the hands of the clock only went forward when she wanted to make them go back. "I must've been in la-la land," she said, shaking her head in disbelief.

Now, at my mention of the clocks, she grew pale again, so I said, "The worst is behind you, Mom."

She took a deep breath, hoping, I could tell, that I was right. As a general rule, I wasn't.

THE NEXT FEW DAYS proved every bit as rough as predicted. "I feel like I'm coming out of my skin" was how my mother put it. Clothes were insupportable, so she stayed in her nightgown and robe all day long. Unable to get comfortable, she moved between rooms like the ghost of someone who'd died a sudden, violent death. The girls, though glad their grandmother was recovering, were also grateful that their restaurant jobs got them out of the house. Barbara and I had no such refuge, and at the end of each day we huddled in our bed in the apartment above the garage, out of earshot for a few hours and thankful she couldn't possibly negotiate the stairs. By the end of the week, though, her appetite returned, and she was clearly feeling better. She thought maybe the time had come to return to Woodland Hills. Her doctor agreed. So did Barbara. So did I.

The first thing she saw when she entered the apartment, as if for the first time, was the piece of paper on which she'd scratched *8:45* and then *REAL TIME*. I couldn't tell what scared her more, the message itself or that her beautiful Palmer Method handwriting was a barely legible scrawl. She pulled one of the chairs out from the dinette and sat down in it heavily, suddenly drained. The plan had been to take inventory of her kitchen, make a list of everything she'd need, and hit the supermarket, but I could tell she was done for the day.

"Is it too soon?" I said, trying to imagine what it must be like to return to a "home" she hadn't yet lived in and couldn't remember.

She shook her head. "I have to do it sometime."

"How about we make out a small list of stuff for the next day or two, and I'll go to the store? We can save the big order for later in the week."

"Whatever," she said, and paused. "Do you honestly think Mark saved my life?"

"I'm certain of it."

She was staring at the refrigerator now. "What am I supposed to do with all those frozen dinners?" A true child of the Depression, she hated few things more than wasting food.

"It's not that you can't have frozen dinners anymore," I reminded her. "Just that you have to eat some other things, too."

"No," she said, never one for half measures. "We'll toss them out." Next she turned her attention to the living room. "You did such a nice job with my books. You know just where everything goes. It's perfect."

We both knew it wasn't, of course. Over the next days and weeks, she'd find things that were out of place and rearrange them, making them, as she liked to put it, "just right." But she wanted to pay me a compliment, and I was pleased to accept it.

What she said then surprised me. "Do you think I'll ever be able to read again?"

She hadn't read anything at our house, which was predictable if you thought about it at all. How can you read when you can't sit still? Worse, there wasn't much inducement, our shelves sagging under the weight of Anita Brookner and her truth-telling ilk. What my mother really wanted to know wasn't whether she'd be able to read again but if that could ever again be a reliable means of escape. At the possibility that it might not, I felt my own spirits plummet in sympathetic dread.

She looked around aimlessly once again, though in a new way. "I hate it here," she said sadly. "I'm sorry. I wish I didn't, but I do."

Though normally I'd have pointed out that she hadn't been there long enough to render such a judgment, I was weary of such futile nonsense. She *was* going to hate it, and we both knew it. "We'll keep your name on the other lists," I assured her.

Actually, I'd driven by Megunticook House when she was in the hospital and noticed the exterior was being painted, so

I stopped by and added her name to their list as well. (Later in the year a vacancy would come up, and this time my mother loved the place. In fact, the painting had transformed it so completely that she insisted I'd never taken her there before. She would've remembered, she said, because it was perfect, *just* what we'd been looking for, *so* much better than Woodland Hills.)

"You look exhausted," she said now, taking my hand. "What a long haul this has been for you."

I started to say that it'd been a tough few days, all right, but then realized she was going all the way back to Arizona, maybe even to Helwig Street. "I just wish you could be happy, Mom."

"I *used* to be," she sighed, and in her inflection was the same profound mystification I'd heard the week before when she asked me to explain why, despite her formidable will, the hands of the clock would only go in one direction. "I know you don't believe that, but I was."

Here and There

IT WOULD'VE TAKEN about forty minutes to drive out-island from Edgartown in the summer, but in late December, with so few tourists on the island and no mopeds or cyclists clogging the narrow, two-lane roads, it took about half that long. To me, the winter landscape was starkly beautiful, but I found myself wondering if my mother would agree. Given that the alternatives were Gloversville and coastal Maine, she'd wholeheartedly embraced the idea of scattering her ashes in Menemsha Pond, a place the rest of us would regularly visit, but today it wasn't hard to imagine her taking one look at the frigid, windswept, gunmetal-gray landscape and saying, *What an awful, awful place.* Was the island simply the last in a series of wrong places for her? Is that what the previous night's dream, in which I'd carried her through the streets of that nameless town in search of an unknown destination, was trying to tell me?

Emily and Kate both planned to speak at this interment, and driving out there I found myself wondering what they'd say. Their approaches to dealing with my mother had always been different, Emily infinitely patient and loving and accommodating, Kate deeply sympathetic to her isolation and loneliness but far less able to surrender to her unreason. In Illinois, when they were still young and Barbara and I had obligations at the university or just needed a night out, my mother had been their occasional babysitter. Once we were out the door, the three of them would caucus in the living room and decide on a theme for the evening's entertainment, after which, while my mother watched TV or read, the girls would raid my wife's closet for costumes, practice their lines in their bedrooms, then stage a play or musical for my mother's edification and critical evaluation. Both girls had fond memories of such evenings, of having the undivided attention of an appreciative adult, though things had changed by the time we moved to Maine. As teenagers, they weren't so malleable or as easily delighted. More important, by then the roles were reversed. On those rare occasions when Barbara and I both had to be absent for a few days, my mother would come over to the Waterville house to look after them, but they both understood without having to be told that it was their responsibility to keep an eye on her. We'd tried hard not to undermine their affection for their grandmother, but of course they'd borne witness to her mood swings and meltdowns, not to mention our difficulties in keeping her relatively calm and stable.

Though they'd been told a good deal about my mother as

a young woman, her yearning for a life of dancing and clever repartee and nice clothes and personal freedom, the old GE photo we found after her death had knocked both girls for a loop, and I knew they were still trying to reconcile it with the grandmother who later in life made them sit still when they visited her apartment and instructed them not to touch anything; whose shirts and slacks and sweaters hung in the closet sheathed in plastic, nothing allowed to touch anything else for fear of wrinkles; whose refrigerator reflected the same obsessive distance, the milk carton always a respectful three inches from the orange juice. As a young woman, my mother had in many ways been ahead of her time, determined to make it on her own in a man's world. Back then, GE was almost exclusively male, and the men she'd worked for and with had both accepted and admired her. In this respect she wasn't so different from the brave, trailblazing women our daughters had studied in their college courses, who helped to institute workplace reform and equal-pay-for-equal-work legislation. How could this woman in the photo be the same person who'd lectured them so tirelessly, and often inappropriately, on highly conservative gender roles (*This is what the man does* and *That is what the woman does*). To prepare them for marriage, my mother had given them to understand that in every relationship, one partner or the other had to rule the roost, and that in good marriages the roost was ruled by the rooster. As the girls grew older, it became clear to her that these lectures were falling on deaf ears. Kate in particular worried her, and my mother had warned us throughout her adolescence that we were allowing her to grow up headstrong, that her unflinching independence was decidedly unfeminine. In the end, despite having fewer sharp temperamental edges and always lavishing on her grandmother such generous forbearance, Emily fared little better. When she fell in love with Steve, our shy, brilliant son-in-law-to-be, my mother wondered out loud if he'd be man enough to tame and rule her. ("I suppose I could slap you around a little," he'd offered, when Emily reported this concern to him, "if that would make her feel any better.")

We'd timed our arrival for sunset. Tom, Kate's husband, a talented photographer, had brought along a camera to document an occasion whose exact nature we'd not discussed, preferring spontaneity. Menemsha, a hive of activity in season, was deserted now, which suited us fine given that what we intended, though unscripted and benign, was quite possibly illegal. A few fishing vessels bobbed in the swell against a nearby dock, and every now and then a voice or two would be borne in on the wind. Somewhere out in the harbor a buoy clanged, surely the loneliest sound in the world. A pickup truck rumbled by, its driver leaning forward for a better view of six well-dressed out-of-towners congregated at the water's edge. It wouldn't have required much imagination for the fellow to guess our purpose, though I suspect he'd have been surprised to learn that the person whose ashes we meant to scatter had been to the island only once, for a single week some fifty years before, determined to show the little boy she had in tow that beauty existed in the world.

With the sun hovering a few inches above the western horizon, I clambered down, urn in hand, over jagged rocks that were wet and slippery with moss to where the water was lapping the shore, thinking to myself that it would be about right if I broke my ass trying to accomplish one last foolish thing on my mother's behalf. Not much is left of a human professionally reduced by heat and flame, and it took me just a few seconds to scatter that biblical dust in the churning waves, where it swiftly mingled with sand and silt and tiny pebbles. By the time I scrambled back up the embankment, the sun was sitting on the western waves, large and red but without the power to warm. Emily spoke first, thanking her grandmother for the gift of this island that over the years had played such a magical role in the lives of our whole family; then Kate recalled with bittersweet affection her grandmother's ability to imagine vividly a happier, better future, even if she couldn't quite see herself in it. When they were done, I read the Shakespeare sonnet that begins "Fear no more the heat o' the Sun," partly because it was appropriate to the occasion and one of the most beautiful poems in the language, but also because I hoped it might hide from my loved ones the fact that I myself had nothing to say, that while part of me was here with them on this beloved shore, another part was wandering, as it had been for months, in a barren, uninhabited landscape not unlike the one in my dream. I realized I'd felt like this for a while. Though life had gone on since my mother's death—Kate had gotten married, I'd finally published another book and gone on tour with it— some sort of internal-pause button had been pushed, allowing another part of me, one I'd specifically kept sequestered to deal with my mother, to fall silent. Since her death, Barbara and I had gone through all her things and settled her affairs, but we'd barely spoken of her. After thirty-five years, for the first time, we were alone in our marriage, and neither of us seemed to have the heart to discuss what that meant. There might have been more to say if the girls had been around, but Emily was living in Amherst and Kate in London, and the rest of my family still in upstate New York.

We therefore scheduled a family memorial service for the following summer in Gloversville, the sort of gathering my mother would've liked—just family and friends and food and swapping stories, like the one about the Christmas when she, all dressed up, was trapped astraddle a snowbank, everybody laughing too hard to help her get unstuck. But in the meantime, not much had been said; and when you say nothing, it speaks volumes.

The last year of my mother's life had been particularly grueling. The specialist who'd diagnosed her congestive heart failure had explained how things would likely go over the year or possibly two that remained to her. Given how hard her heart was now working, she might suffer a major heart attack, but it was far more likely that her decline would be gradual. For a while, at least, she'd continue to feel sluggish and tired, nothing more. Over time, though, she'd be increasingly short of breath, especially when she exerted herself. Every now and then there'd be days when she'd feel better, even energetic, her breathing less labored, and he advised her to stick with her normal routines for as long as she could, to continue her weekly trips to the supermarket and to the hairdresser. Eventually, however, her good days would be fewer and farther between; she'd become housebound, then bedridden. Toward the end she'd require morphine, not for pain, but to make her breathing easier. I was the one choking back sobs as the doctor delivered this grim prognosis. My mother accepted it with near-perfect equanimity. She was being told what would happen, not what might, and certainty never frightened her, even certain catastrophe. She wasn't scared to die. As we drove home, she actually comforted me.

Living, on the other hand, in the greater scheme of things a relentless march of inconsequential minutiae, continued over the ensuing weeks and months to generate crises. Appearances, as always, weighed far more heavily on her decisions than they should have. No doubt recalling the enormous oxygen tank that stood sentry behind my grandfather's chair on Helwig Street, the one my grandmother used to glare at homicidally every time he got up to leave the room, muttering "Ugly" beneath her breath, my mother wasn't anxious to start on oxygen. Her living room was arranged just so, to accentuate her "pretties," the menagerie of small, ornate objects (a ballerina, a cut-glass bowl, etc.) she'd been collecting down through the years, and a few were given pride of place on the sill, where they made it difficult to open or close the windows. As the perimeter of her world continued to contract, it was imperative for her to keep control over what remained, and an oxygen tank, unsightly and utilitarian, represented a serious breach of taste. Of course the technology had come a long way, and the small, boxlike oxygen machine we eventually rented could be tucked away behind an end table, but that didn't matter; she knew it was there, unwanted, a violation. We also got her a small, portable tank for when she needed to leave the house, but she'd seen people out in public with such unwieldy contraptions, and she didn't want to be one of them. She would use it when she came to our house, but refused to be seen in stores or restaurants with a breathing apparatus. The plastic tubing, once inserted, made her nose look like a pig's snout, or so she claimed, and she couldn't bear to be seen looking like that. Hearing she was ill, people at Megunticook House were concerned, but after going on oxygen, she let it be known that she didn't want visitors, even people she liked. And so, in short order, her world shrank to her own two rooms, the apartment of her one good friend across the hall and, when she was feeling up to it, our house across town.

For what seemed like a very long time, my own world wasn't much larger. With few exceptions, I declined speaking engagements and canceled personal appearances. Except for visiting our daughters in London and Amherst, we stuck close to home. Faced with an undefined period of staggering health-care expenses, I hunkered down with the novel I was working on, while Barbara, who'd recently gotten her real-estate license, kept busy learning the ropes of a new profession. For a while I did most of what needed doing—shopping for my mother's groceries, making small repairs in the apartment, taking care of trash and recycling—but before long it became necessary to hire professionals to help with more intimate duties.

Moving her in with us was something I refused to even consider because it would have made a nurse of my wife, and besides, what my mother seemed most adamant about was keeping things just as they were for as long as possible, especially her apartment, so I promised to make that happen.

Even in terminal illness, her emotional cycles continued, exacerbated now by physical ones that proceeded as expected and predicted. There were good days and bad days, and it was the good ones we all came to fear. On bad days, when her energy level was low, her breathing difficult, my mother fussed and found fault less. On bad days her Meals on Wheels were a godsend, the people who delivered them saints. When listless, she understood she was too ill to be left alone, that she needed help with almost everything, even getting up from the sofa to go to the bathroom. On days when she woke up feeling better, though, watch out. Then the Meals on Wheels were inedible, and (again, shades of Woody Allen) the portions inadequate. When a delivery was running late, she'd call and tell them not to bother; when it came anyway, she wouldn't ring whoever was bringing it into the building. The health-care workers, who'd all been warned, bore the brunt of it when she went on the warpath. Some quit. Others—several of whom she'd taken an aversion to at first sight—she refused to let in the door. She knew as her condition deteriorated that she was becoming increasingly dependent on them, but on good days she couldn't see why people who most of the time just sat and watched television with her were paid so much. We'd never discussed what these costs amounted to, but she knew it was expensive and not covered by Medicare, which was partly why she was so unreasonable on this subject. To her way of thinking, to justify such expense, the people we hired should always be working, vacuuming or scrubbing the bathtub, as if they were maids with medical training. Did they have to be in the apartment with her when they weren't needed? Couldn't they wait out in the hall? Couldn't she ring for them? "Maybe you don't care if you're getting ripped off," she said whenever I tried to explain what their duties were and weren't, "but I do."

That spring, before we went to London for a few days to visit Kate, we planned our absence, hour by hour, with Vickie, who ran the health-care service, making sure my mother's days and evenings were all covered. Night had become a particular bone of contention. Not long after she was diagnosed, she'd gotten a push-button necklace that would summon help in case of an accident, but she didn't want anybody in her apartment overnight. Only after intense negotiation did she reluctantly agree to have someone stay for the duration of our London trip. I was still worried, so we came up with a contingency plan. If she took a turn for the worse in the run-up to our departure, I'd remain behind. For a while it looked like that's what was going to happen, but after a string of bad days she rallied, and her doctor assured us that she'd be stable until we returned. I called one last time from the airport to make sure, but she swore everything was fine. The night person had just arrived, and they were watching TV. I should go and have a good time. Something in her voice gave me pause, though, and when we landed at Heathrow seven hours later, I wasn't surprised to find there was a message on my cell from Vickie. My mother had waited until we were safely onboard our plane, then fired everybody.

A month later she had a minor heart attack that put her in the hospital, and things got even worse. She claimed the recommended regimen of physical therapy was simply too difficult to do, though the nurses said she'd never so much as tried. They'd also recommended what they made the mistake of referring to as "psychological therapy." I explained that this was all about rethinking how, after you'd suffered a heart attack, you rose from a chair and got out of bed in the morning, but my mother was having none of it. There was nothing wrong with her head, and she knew perfectly well how to get out of a chair. Which left the hospital staff little choice but to return her to Megunticook House, where it soon became apparent she was going to need a lot more care. Whether she liked it or not, somebody had to be there at night to help her get to the bathroom. The problem was that of all the workers sent from the agency to help her, she liked only a couple. They of course had families and lives of their own, and there were more hours in the week than any two people could cover. Shift changes were especially problematic. My mother particularly hated falling asleep with one caregiver in the next room, then waking up to another the next morning. Moreover, she didn't want the night attendant to stretch out on her sofa, fearing for its springs. "It wasn't *made* for people to sleep on," she complained, "especially not obese Mainers." I tried to catch her caregivers near the end of their shifts, in part so they could bring me up to speed on what had transpired but also to find out how badly they'd been abused and insulted and to apologize. They were no sooner out the door than my mother would use what little remained of her failing heart and lungs to berate those she considered lazy or stupid and to bemoan the fact that her favorites weren't always available. Vickie, she believed, was saving all the good ones for her favored clients, whose families insisted on top-quality care.

There were times when I seriously considered wringing her neck, but then the cycle would end, and there she'd be again, my mother, lost and frail and afraid, with barely enough energy to draw her next breath, her heart a sledgehammer in her chest—anxious, it seemed, for this terrible struggle to be over. In the weeks before she entered the hospital for the last time, she couldn't get comfortable. In the living room she'd struggle to her feet and announce that she couldn't stand it there any longer and was going to bed early. I should go home. (By this time I was visiting, literally, morning, noon, and night.) But twenty minutes later she'd emerge from the bedroom saying she couldn't bear lying down, that sitting up was better. In addition to sapping what little strength remained, these short journeys were also treacherous. Forgetting she was tethered to the oxygen machine, she often managed to tangle her long lead of plastic tubing when she went around corners, pulling it free of her nose, which she sometimes didn't notice or immediately realize was why she suddenly couldn't fill her lungs. Back and forth she went, ninety pounds of pure will and desperation, life reduced to purposeless, exhausting motion, until another heart attack, after which even that tortured, senseless motion became impossible.

MORPHINE. A BLESSING. During the last month of my mother's life in the hospice wing at the hospital, the drug did its almost-mystical business of protecting the self from itself, of relaxing her so that she could "breathe easier" both literally and metaphorically. Under its influence her features sometimes unclenched, allowing me to glimpse in the tiny, mummified figure in her hospital bed the confident, lovely, brave young woman I'd known as a boy. When a new dose was administered, she'd smile and slip under the wave, and often, exhausted, I'd follow her down, falling asleep in my chair as if I, too, were connected to the drip. At other times, powerful though it was, even morphine failed to vanquish the anxiety that had come to rule her life, and then her eyes would grow small and hard with concentrated terror and defiance, the old, unwinnable battle still raging on. I tried to calm her by saying I was right there at the foot of the bed and promising I wouldn't go anywhere. But knowing she wasn't afraid of death, I was curious, as well, and asked more than once what was scaring her so. "That things, you know . . . ," she'd begin, but having gotten that far, she'd grow confused and frustrated.

"Can you explain?" I persisted, hoping that, even at this late date, if she could just articulate her fear, I might be able to help her dispel it.

"You know," she said, as if she suspected I'd somehow forgotten something I knew perfectly well, that I could summon the memory if I just concentrated hard enough. "That things . . . you know . . . won't . . ."

"Won't *what,* Mom?"

"You know," she insisted, smiling weakly now, "won't turn out right."

MY MOTHER WASN'T the only one confused and disoriented those final weeks. Meaning to visit her, I'd often drive over to Megunticook House, realizing only after I'd pulled in to the parking lot and turned off the ignition that she wasn't there anymore.

One night not long after she moved into the hospital's hospice wing, I went home early and fell into a deep, dreamless slumber from which I was awakened, bewildered and panicked, when the telephone rang a few minutes before midnight.

"Rick?" she said, perhaps not recognizing my sleep-thick voice.

Had I forgotten, I wondered, to go over to her apartment after dinner?

"Rick?"

"Mom?" I said. "What is it?"

"I need you to come."

"Mom, it's midnight," I said, staring stupidly at the clock on the nightstand. Had five whole hours passed? How was that possible?

"I pressed the button."

"What button, Mom?"

"For the nurse. Ten minutes ago. She never came."

"She will," I told her. Barbara put a hand on my shoulder and rested her forehead on the back of my neck. "Be patient."

"It's you I need."

"I'll see you in the morning. I promise."

Silence on the line, then. Had she hung up? No, she was back, needing me to understand. "It's terrible here," she said. "You have no idea."

IT'S YOU I NEED . . . it's terrible here.

Seven small words, but embedded in them, somewhere, is the reason that a man who makes his living with words isn't able to offer any when Emily and Kate finish speaking. The closure that death is supposed to bring has somehow eluded me, which must be why in last night's dream I was carrying my mother toward that unknown destination and why it felt like I'd be doing so forever. Although it's been several months since her death, when the phone rings in the middle of the night, I still expect to hear her voice on the other end of the line, wanting to know where I am, why I've abandoned her.

It's terrible here. I've belatedly come to understand that for my mother *here* was really the place inside her head where everything played on an endless loop. *There* was the place she never stopped trying to get to, where she'd be happy. *Don't I deserve a life?* She must have asked my grandfather this before me, the question serving as explanation for why she was leaving Helwig Street for Arizona. How had he answered it? He'd served in two world wars and was exhausted and slowly strangling, his lungs full of leather dust. I can imagine him telling her that nobody, including her, was entitled to anything, but of course I wasn't there and he might well have said nothing of the sort. She never asked me if I minded her tagging along. She just told me about the job awaiting her in Phoenix and painted a vivid picture for me of the new, free life she'd have when we arrived, leaving me to challenge her right to it.

Or am I misremembering? Did she ask me, and I just forgot? It's possible. That I honestly can't recall something so important seems right, somehow. The mechanism of human destiny—that intricate weave of chance and fate and free will, as distinctly individual as a fingerprint—is surely meant to remain life's central mystery, to resist transparency, to make blame a dangerous and unsatisfactory exercise. I don't blame my mother for anything, certainly not for her ongoing unhappiness, any more than I take pride in having managed to parlay the same genetic character traits that bedeviled her—stubbornness, defiance, an inclination to obsess, an excess of will, a potentially dangerous need to see things my own way—into a rich and satisfying career.

It's you I need. From the time I was a boy I understood that my mother's health, her well-being, was in my hands. How often over the years did she credit me, or my proximity, with restoring her to health? *My rock,* as she was so fond of saying, always there when she needed me most. My own experience, however, had yielded a different truth—that I could easily make things worse, but never better. Or at least not better enough. I was, just as she said, always there, but to me that meant always failing, never being able to cure what ailed her. I could help her step back from the precipice and restore the status quo, but the status quo was neither health nor happiness.

Now, standing with my family in the deepening dark, I feel profoundly what a terrible mistake she made in trusting me, in believing that we were cut from the same cloth, that one day I'd see things as she did, that given time I'd grow into the soul-mate role that she'd planned for me. She seemed not to grasp that I'm by nature a problem solver, that I'm fundamentally optimistic and believe most problems have solutions. When she asked me if she didn't deserve a life like anybody else, she probably thought of it as a rhetorical question. Who would deny another human being the right to a life? She couldn't have known that I'd take it as a riddle I was supposed to figure out, a problem that had a solution I'd eventually discover if I just kept looking, that I'd never give up.

But of course I now realize that isn't quite true. At some point along the spectrum of what we like to think of as "real time," I simply flatlined and, without admitting it to myself, conceded defeat and started just going through the motions. This was why my dreams were haunted. Because I'd given up on someone I loved, someone who'd never, ever, given up on me. I couldn't speak because the only thing left to say was *I'm sorry,* and the person I needed to say it to was gone.

High and Dry

AFTER THE VINEYARD, Barbara and I could feel the pendulum begin to swing, tragedy waning and comedy, at least in the Shakespearean sense, waxing. Kate and Tom had gotten married in London back in November, and we were now again in the nuptial mode, preparing for Emily's in September. Caught up in the spirit of these proceedings, I started work on a wedding story. At least I thought it was a story. It turned out to be a novel, though, one that was cleaved right down the center, a wedding anchoring each half. Compared with the book that preceded it—my darkest, written and revised during my mother's long, final descent—this new novel was a breezy tale that seemed to suggest I was finding my way back to the cautious, hard-won optimism that characterizes my fiction. Back on the Vineyard I'd feared that my nightmare—about carrying my mother through unfamiliar streets toward an unknown destination—might be a recurring one, but I hadn't had it since, and I took this to mean that my mother was finally at rest, or perhaps that I was. It seems strange to admit it now, but just being alive was at some level surprising. In contrast to the remarkable longevity of the women on my mother's side of the family, Russo males had a piss-poor track record, and somewhere in the back of my mind I must've linked my mother's chronological destiny with my own. Yet here I was, not only alive but, according to my doctor, in excellent health.

So Barbara and I started making plans. After all, our circumstances had changed dramatically. Suddenly we had neither ailing parents nor heart-stopping medical bills. Our daughters' educations were paid for. By autumn both girls would be married to the kind of young men we'd hardly dared to hope for, and all four young people were embarking on careers they were passionate about. Which begged an obvious question: what in the world were Barbara and I going to do with ourselves? At long last we'd been left to our own devices, only to discover we couldn't recollect precisely what those devices were. Perhaps we'd need all new ones.

One of the things we'd been unable to do while my mother was alive was to travel, at least not together. I could go off on a book tour, or to L.A. or New York for a script meeting, as long as Barbara remained behind to hold down the fort, and of course she could visit her family in Arizona if I stayed put. Now we could actually go places together. For years we'd longed for an apartment in Boston so we wouldn't have to fly out of Portland, Maine, the preferred airport of hijackers and no one else. A place in the city would also give us somewhere to spend the darkest months of Maine's interminable winters. All this was down the road, though. Meanwhile, the theme would be weddings, fictional and real. That felt both right and appropriate. Weddings are all about our hopes for and faith in the future, right? Right.

Except not entirely. As I knew all too well from recent experience, and was learning more about with every new page of my novel-in-progress, weddings are also about the past.

KATE'S WEDDING HAD BEEN HELD at the Royal Society for the Arts, a series of underground vaults, formerly wine cellars, just off the Strand. She and Tom, who's English, would be living in London, so there'd been no question of having the ceremony in the States. The wedding was relatively small: Tom's family; some friends from the Slade Art School, where they'd met; a few of Kate's college friends. Understandably, given the distance and expense, not many family members from our side of the Atlantic made the trip. The exception was my cousin Greg and his wife, Carole, both of whom have always lived in Gloversville. "Quite a ways from Helwig Street," Greg said, taking in the venue. It wasn't as grand as "Royal Society" might suggest, but the arching brick vaults, candlelit for the occasion, were impressive. There's nothing remotely like it in an upstate mill town. The person who would've appreciated it the most, of course, was my mother.

While we waited for the bride and groom to finish having

their photos taken, the how-far-we'd-all-come theme occupied the American contingent. Nat Sobel, my friend and literary agent, immediately took to my cousin, telling Greg that as a boy he, too, lived near a tannery that released its toxins into the local stream, the water running a different color each day depending on the dye batch. And so, flutes of Prosecco in hand, we began swapping stories about the worst jobs we'd ever had.

I recalled my brief nonunion construction job in Johnstown. Other summers I'd been able to get union work at an hourly rate nearly twice what men were making at the skin mills. That year, though, jobs were scarce, and I hadn't gotten one. Nonunion construction was a different world. The first week we had to drill holes in a concrete abutment, not a difficult task if you have a drill. We didn't. What we did have was a jackhammer and a foreman who was unconstrained by conventional thinking. The jackhammer guy and I formed a team that afternoon. Balancing his weapon on my shoulder, I held on for dear life as we jacked horizontally into the wall, sharp shards of concrete blasting back into our faces. Another thing we didn't have was a spare set of goggles.

This story will win a lot of bad-job contests unless your competitor has worked in the beam house of a skin mill doing the wettest, foulest, lowest-paid, and most dangerous work in the whole tannery. Greg had worked in one for a couple months one summer, and his younger brother, Jim, for much longer. The first and probably nastiest job in the beaming operation was unloading the skins, which arrived at the loading dock on railroad cars, still reeking of the slaughterhouse.

The word *skin* probably gives the wrong impression. Most people have never seen a hide—sheep, pig, calf, cow—unattached from its living owner. Stretched out flat it's big and, especially with cows, surprisingly heavy. (Our grandfather gave himself a hernia tugging hides from one position to another over his cutting table.) When the skin arrived in the beam house, the top side was still covered with coarse hair, the underside with patches of maggot-infested flesh and gristle. The stench? You don't want to know, but imagine—if you can—what it must be like to spend an eight-hour shift unloading a railcar full of them in extreme temperatures.

Later, inside the beam house, Greg assured us, things got even worse. Here the skins were submerged in huge vats and soaked for days in a chemical bath that stripped off most of the hair and the last of the clinging flesh. Naturally, these chemicals could easily do the same to hair on the hands and forearms of men who hoisted the soaked skins out of the vats, so long rubber gloves were issued. You'd think the skins would be lighter minus the hair and flesh, but you'd be wrong, because untanned skins reabsorb the moisture lost during transport and this cleansing. The soaking also turns the heavy skins slippery. The rubber gloves make the slick skins harder to grab hold of, as does the fact that you're bent over the vat and standing on a wet concrete floor.

At some point, like the men farther down the line who prod the tanned skins into staking machines and roller presses, you'll do what you know you shouldn't: you will take off the rubber gloves, because that immediately makes the job easier.

At the end of your shift you'll wash your hands and arms vigorously with the coarsest soap you can find, and when you get home you'll do it again. You'll gradually lose the hair on your hands and forearms, but otherwise, for a while, everything seems fine. Okay, sometimes your fingers itch. A little at first, then a lot. Your skin begins to feel odd, almost loose, as if moisture has somehow gotten beneath it and what you're trying to scratch isn't on the surface. Finally it itches so bad you can't stand it anymore, and you grab your thumb or forefinger and give the skin a twist, then a pull. The skin, several layers of it, comes away in one piece, like the finger of a latex glove. (On the other side of the Atlantic, at the Royal Society for the Arts, my cousin demonstrated with his thumb, everybody wincing as he pulled off the imaginary prophylactic of skin.) Instantly, the itching becomes stinging pain as the air impinges on your raw flesh. Later, someone comes around with a jar of black goop and you plunge your raw thumb into it, the coolness offering at least some relief, and for a while you go back to wearing the rubber gloves.

This is only the beginning, though, just the beam house's way of saying hello when all you want to say is good-bye—to the skins, the foul chemical air, even your coworkers, because let's face it, the ones who've been at it for a while, many of them with fifth-grade educations, aren't quite right. You all make the same shitty pay, but at the end of the summer you get to go back to college, and for that the others hate you. Meanwhile, you can't imagine getting used to work like this, or that the day will ever come when the lunch whistle sounds and instead of going outside into the fresh air you'll decide it's easier to just stay where you are, take a seat on a pallet of decomposing hides, wipe your hands on your pants, and eat your sandwich right there—because what the hell, it's been forever since you could really smell or taste anything anyway. Plus, in the beam house there's entertainment. You can watch the rats chase the terrified cats that have been introduced to hunt them.

As my cousin related this story, which I was hearing for the first time, I became conscious of being in two places at once. I had one dry, wing-tipped foot in the candlelit world of a fancy arts society in London in 2007; the other work-booted foot was sloshing through the wet, slippery beam-house floor in Gloversville, New York, circa 1970. That younger me wasn't a novelist, or even a husband or a father. He was just a twenty-year-old whose future could be stolen from him, who might indeed be complicit in the theft, because I remembered vividly how sometimes, late in August, working road construction with my father, my body lean and hard from the summer's labor, I'd think about not going back to school. I could live with my grandparents on Helwig Street and do that hard, honest work my father and his friends did all year-round. The wing-tipped me, now holding an empty champagne flute, felt a sudden crushing guilt, as if to be where I was I must've cheated destiny or, worse, swapped destinies with some other poor sod. I felt my throat constrict dangerously, though I couldn't tell if that was due to my cousin's story or because the wedding party—with Kate absolutely radiant in the first hour of her marriage, and Emily laughing her throaty laugh and looping her arm through her fiancé's—had at this moment returned. Two smart, confident, beautiful young women, their feet planted squarely in the candlelit world before them, on *this* day—for them, at least—the only one that existed. The time might come when they, too, would feel haunted, guilty about what they'd been spared in life, keenly aware of how things, but for the grace of God, might have gone otherwise. But that day seemed a long way off.

"More Prosecco?" one of the waiters inquired.

"Yes, please," I told her, holding out my glass. Gloversville, I reminded myself, was on the other side of the world. "Absolutely. Lay it on me. Right to the brim."

UNTIL WE BEGAN PLANNING Emily's wedding we didn't fully comprehend how easily we'd gotten off with Kate's. We'd feared a London wedding would be a logistical nightmare, but being on the other side of the Atlantic had the unintended consequence of lowering everyone's expectations, at least of us. Nobody assumed we would deal with day-to-day details and crises. Tom's parents stepped up. Decisions got made without us. We showed up. We wrote the check.

By contrast, Emily's wedding was larger and would take place in Camden, where a matrimonial clusterfuck like the one I was gleefully imagining in my new novel would long be remembered. With no ocean to protect us, our very different families showed up en masse. Barbara's Arizona contingent, none of them seasoned travelers, needed assistance at every juncture. My own Gloversville squad wasn't much better, but at least they'd be arriving by car. And of course there was our future son-in-law's family and friends to consider. Add to all this the normal wedding anxieties about who, for personal reasons, should be kept well clear of whom, and what would happen if the Red Staters were allowed too close proximity to the Blue. When the whole thing threatened to overwhelm us, we reminded ourselves that our tribulations would have been multiplied exponentially if my mother had been alive.

Truth be told, Barbara and Emily handled most of the wedding arrangements while I forged ahead with the book I hoped would pay for them. About this time I had a few odd dreams about my mother in which she telephoned from Europe, wanting to know why I'd abandoned her there and when I was coming to get her. These made me wary, but they were too comic—Europe? my dead mother was calling from Europe?—to be truly unsettling. Otherwise, I thought I was doing pretty well, certainly better than my novel's protagonist, Jack Griffin. At the book's outset he'd been heading to the first wedding on Cape Cod with an urn containing his father's ashes in the right wheel well of his trunk; now, driving to the second wedding, this one in Maine, he'd added his mother's urn to the left. Poor Jack, I thought. Scattering my own mother's ashes hadn't been easy, but my character seemed utterly unequal to this fairly straightforward task. Death had made his mother even more loquacious than she'd been in life, even more deter-mined to insinuate herself into his life and marriage, both of which were coming apart. A terrible snob of an English professor, she was (to me, if not to him) wonderfully entertaining, in part because she was about as different as anyone could be from my own mother. Nor was Jack, despite superficial similarities of age and profession, all that temperamentally similar to me. And so far as I knew, my own marriage wasn't failing. All of which allowed me to believe, as a writer must, that I was writing fiction, not thinly veiled autobiography.

IT WAS AROUND this time that a large padded envelope arrived in my mailbox bearing a Gloversville postmark, never a welcome sign. Inside were two books, the first a copy of my novel *Bridge of Sighs*. The man who sent it in hopes of an autograph was a judge named Vincent DeSantis, who, except for college and law school, had spent his life in Gloversville, and who, as he explained in the accompanying letter, had strongly identified with Lucy Lynch, the book's protagonist, who'd done the same thing. Clearly he thought he was writing to Lucy's friend Robert Noonan, an artist who in the novel flees their boyhood town, never to return. I couldn't really blame him, given how infrequently I go back to Gloversville.

The other book in the padded envelope was *Toward Civic Integrity: Re-establishing the Micropolis,* written by, well, Vincent DeSantis, and seeing this my heart sank, as it always does when I'm sent books I haven't asked for with a view toward my endorsement. But Mr. DeSantis wasn't looking for a blurb, and his book, despite its rather scholarly title, wasn't an esoteric work of nonfiction. It was about Gloversville, and the question he posed was whether it and similar communities had a future in the global twenty-first century or were in inevitable and irreversible decline. "All is not lost in your hometown," the author assured me. "A network of dedicated and talented individuals has lately been working to reassemble the pieces of this fractured micropolis." My knee-jerk reaction to this Humpty Dumpty sentiment was *Yeah, right. All the king's horses and all the king's men* . . . I tossed the book on a tall stack of volumes whose common denominator was that I was unlikely to read them in this or any other lifetime. Not interested.

Yet that wasn't quite true. Since Kate's wedding my cousin's beam-house stories had been in my thoughts. I was also worried about Greg himself. A few years earlier he'd had open-heart surgery to replace a malfunctioning valve, but he still couldn't sleep very well lying down and was getting by on a couple hours a night. Though I'd tried to keep in touch, when I inquired about his health he always put me off with his standard line, "Nah, I'm doing great for an old guy." Then we'd talk about what our kids were up to and what movies we'd seen and whether I was working on something new. And eventually the talk would turn to Gloversville: who'd been jailed or diagnosed, who'd gone into a nursing home or died. When I mentioned I couldn't get his beam-house experiences out of my head, he launched into a litany of Gloversville woe with which I was all too familiar: men mangled by machines or slowly poisoned or killed in accidents. The three guys who worked the spray line in one mill all dying of the same exotic testicular cancer, a case so outrageous it made the *New York Times*. Then there was the retarded boy hired to clean out the blues room, so named because the chrome used to tan the skins turned them blue. The world of leather is full of scraps—strips of worthless skin and hoof and tail—and every now and then these have to be disposed of and the whole lethal place, including its giant vats, swamped out. One evening, when this kid didn't come home, his mother called the shop to see if he was still around. No, she was told, everybody from the day shift had left. The following morning her son was found lying on the blues room's floor, asphyxiated by fumes. Another man, nearing retirement age, was working a press when his partner inadvertently stepped on the pedal that starts the rollers, catching the man's hand— more like a fin, now—in the mechanism. Yet another day, when it was unseasonably cold on the floor, the foreman sent a man to fire up a boiler that hadn't been inspected in twenty years, and it promptly blew up, killing him. Stories upon stories, each reminding my cousin of other men who died, their families uncompensated. Some dated back to my grandfather's days, ones I'd heard so many times I knew them as well as Greg did, but I understood why he needed to repeat them. The guys who lived this life in this world are, like World War II veterans, mostly gone. Somebody *should* give a shit.

But why me? Hanging up after such conversations with my cousin, I'd find I was roiling with rage I wasn't at all sure I was entitled to. Obviously, I'd never spent a minute in the beam house. Unlike my cousin Jim, on hot summer days I don't have to lance with a needle the hard pustules that still form on my hands, thirty years after the fact. What right does one who'd fled at the earliest opportunity have to speak for those who remained behind? If Vincent DeSantis isn't pissed, why should I be?

NOT LONG AFTER Emily was married, I finished my wedding novel, at the last minute pulling poor Jack Griffin back from the drain he'd been circling. His parents' ashes finally scattered, he was able to make a grudging peace with his past and live again in the present. The book came out and sold well enough for Barbara and me to consider getting that apartment in Boston, so when my book tour concluded we started scouting neighborhoods—the North End, which we both loved though it seemed not to offer what we were looking for; the South End, which was wonderful but not well served by the T; the Back Bay, which had little, at least in our view, to recommend it; and a small rectangle of blocks near South Station called the Leather District, which was convenient to both the train station and the Silver Line T that provided a straight shot out to Logan Airport. Emily and Steve were living in Amherst, Kate and Tom in London, and a place in Boston would make visiting both couples easier. Because, alas, we were entering a new world, one where we had to share our newly married daughters. Holidays would now have to be rotated—Christmas at one set of in-laws, Thanksgiving at the other.

That first year Christmas was ours, and we celebrated in Camden. Ten glorious days' worth of long dinners fueled by red wine, followed by card and board games that lasted into

the wee hours and made zombies of us the following morning. Such festivities would have been impossible if my mother
had been alive, which made for an odd mix of emotions, guilt
chief among them. There were times when, to me, at least, she
felt oddly present. *Why,* she seemed to be asking, *had we never
had such good times when I was alive to enjoy them?* Had she ever had
any idea that she was the one who'd been putting a damper
on things? I doubted it. As a young woman she'd always been
the life of the party, and she continued to think of herself in
that role, even forty years after she could no longer play it.
"Remember what *fun* we used to have at Christmas back on
Helwig Street?" she liked to ask, genuinely bewildered that fun
should elude us so completely now.

At the end of the holidays, though, came a surprise. Just
before she and Tom were to return to England, Kate, partly at
his insistence, confessed that she hadn't been doing so well in
London. When she began to explain what was troubling her,
the symptoms she needed to confront, some things came into
focus. At times during their visit she'd seemed strangely on
edge, borderline manic. We'd noticed that when anyone used
the small, communal laptop computer we kept in the kitchen,
she'd leave the room and return only when it was unoccupied.
Over the last nine months, she told us now, certain sounds—
the clacking of a keyboard, for instance—had begun to inspire
in her not just annoyance but also genuine terror. Boarding
the Tube or a London bus, she had to scan the compartment
for laptop users and stay as far away from them as possible.
If somebody pulled out a computer after she was settled, she

had to move. She'd hoped that being home, away from the cacophony of urban sounds that were driving her nuts, would help, but in Camden the problem actually seemed exacerbated. Having done some online research, she thought she'd identified the problem, and she meant to see somebody as soon as she returned to London. For Barbara and me that wasn't soon enough, so with her permission we arranged for Kate to see a well-regarded anxiety specialist in Portland, and it took him about twenty minutes to confirm her self-diagnosis. She suffered from obsessive-compulsive disorder. With appropriate treatment, she would be fine. Without it, he warned, it would eat her alive.

The next day she and Tom left for London with the names of several good therapists there, and we returned to Camden with a newly purchased book on the subject, which I began to read with foreboding that quickly escalated into full-blown horror and roiling nausea. Because right there in the introduction was the long parade of bizarre behaviors I'd been witnessing in my mother since I was a boy: how she always had to keep her possessions arranged "just so," her love of arbitrary rules for their own sake, her need to "even things up" (the same number of folds to the right and left of the middle on her curtain rods), her constant checking on things she'd already checked in order to "be sure," but then continuing to worry anyway. Worse, all this was here defined as mental illness. That, of course, had been my father's amateur diagnosis: "You *do* know your mother's nuts, right?"

But surely his observation wasn't intended to be clinical.

He'd only meant that for the sake of my own sanity I'd do well to accept that my mother was "batty," half a bubble off of plumb, one card shy of a deck, a few rungs short of a ladder. Supply your own comic metaphor. But the language of this book was neither comic nor euphemistic. Here my mother's "nerves" were anxieties and panic attacks. Nor were such distinctions merely semantic. Crippling anxieties and incapacitating panics (unlike nerves) were serious conditions that demanded treatment. Mental illness, like physical illness, first required diagnosis, then appropriate therapy. Kate had already gotten the first and was embarking on the second. My mother had received neither, and the result had been precisely what the Portland anxiety specialist predicted. She'd gradually been eaten alive.

It wasn't a long book, but I found I could read no more than a short chapter at a sitting. Even then I sometimes had to put the book aside for days or weeks before I returned to it. Description after description, case study after case study, and every single one pertinent. How many times, going as far back as Phoenix, had I asked her why she was obsessing over little things when important matters demanded our attention? *Obsessing* was the word I'd actually used, but I was still astonished to encounter it in a medical book about a condition my mother apparently suffered from. And of course it was beyond demoralizing to see that so many of her "idiosyncrasies" were in fact quite common in the literature of obsession, that they were linked in some fashion to a general, irrational fear of contamination, the same broad anxiety that led so many OCD sufferers to indulge in ritual, repetitive hand washing. When

I'd confronted my mother about obsessing over minutiae, I was merely recommending that she act rationally. It never occurred to me that, as this book suggested, she *couldn't,* that something was preventing her and actually holding her reason hostage. In those afflicted by OCD, the book explained, the part of the brain responsible for decision making is thought to be impaired, which is why they have trouble with rational sequencing or, as I referred to it earlier, triage—*this now, that later.*

Also under constant attack is the obsessive's sense of proportion. All her life my mother had a profound aversion to anything yellow, even to flowers that came in that color. Daffodils in particular provoked in her a visceral disgust. Of course healthy people have favorite and least favorite colors. M&M'S all taste the same, but many people irrationally prefer the red ones. Normal people, however, don't *fear* the red ones. They wouldn't cull the red ones or become ill if forced to eat some. Nor would a healthy person come totally unglued if one day her favorite brand of tissue was available only in yellow, as my mother once had in a supermarket. A normal person wouldn't stand paralyzed in the middle of the aisle, quivering with rage and frustration. Yellow made my mother sick to her stomach. She knew it shouldn't and that it didn't do that to other people. But that's what yellow did to her, and how do you argue with a sensation?

Indeed, it's at the level of sensation that an obsessive's anxieties often rule. From the time she was a girl, my mother claimed, she'd had an extraordinarily acute sense of smell. She regarded this as an asset, like twenty-twenty vision, though its consequences were uniformly unpleasant. She considered olive oil a foul, corrupt substance, and no amount of evidence regarding its health benefits could shake that conviction. Back on Helwig Street, when we sat on the front porch on summer evenings, she'd be driven indoors by "vile" smells that only she could detect emanating from a house across the street, where an Italian American family lived. They cooked in *oil,* she explained, her face contorting in revulsion, not butter, like we did. Her obsession with food odors intensified after she left Helwig Street and started living in apartments, where her neighbors were closer to hand, their kitchens on the opposite side of a thin wall. "What's with your mother and all the Air Wicks?" my wife wanted to know the first time we visited her in Phoenix. Even then there'd been air fresheners in every room, two in the bathroom, all opened to the max. Every apartment my mother ever lived in smelled like the inside of a can of Glade.

She was still relatively young when I first began wondering if the smells that tormented her might not have any basis in objective reality. Often the same odor that made her gag seemed to me quite pleasant, if sometimes redolent of spices and herbs she herself never used, such as cumin, coriander, tarragon, and cilantro. More tellingly, the offending aromas always emanated from the apartments of people she didn't like anyway, as was the case with the Helwig Street Italians. In my own house garlic and olive oil came together in the early stages of a great many meals, and for a long time I thought only politeness had prevented my mother from remarking on the same smells there that elsewhere made her ill. Each time she recounted some new tale of oil or garlic wafting across the hall into her apartment, I wondered if this was a hint that I should refrain from using these ingredients whenever she came to dinner. Except in truth it was the exact opposite. Many of her favorite meals, the ones she most often asked for, were heavy with the very ingredients she claimed to loathe.

It also occurred to me that there might be a link between these odor aversions and her lifelong devotion to frozen dinners. Back in Gloversville they'd made sense. At the end of a long workday, why would she want to take the time and trouble to prepare a meal for just herself? Furthermore, as she was always quick to point out, cooking for one was expensive. American food manufacturers packaged their products for families, not single people. But at some point I began to suspect it was really all about the odors, which she maintained were magnified in the small kitchens that were part and parcel of apartment living. Residing as I did in a big house, she gave me to understand (as if I'd never lived in confined quarters), I'd have no way of knowing that. By the time she was middle-aged, though, even her frozen dinners had become problematic, and she often confessed to dreading meals, almost as if the necessity of eating were itself somehow shameful. In her apartment she ate quickly, then immediately rinsed the aluminum container the food came in before crushing it and putting it in the trash. Next she tied off the garbage bag, even if it was only a quarter full, and hurried it out to the Dumpster or the garbage room, because otherwise, she explained, by morning the *stench* would be unbearable. Where other obsessives feared contaminated fluids or dirt, my mother seemed particularly focused on airborne contagion. She lived in terror of common colds, and when she caught one she always claimed to know exactly who'd given it to her. Invariably, the culprit was someone she didn't like.

As dispiriting as it was to recognize my mother on virtually every page of the OCD book, it was even more painful to recognize myself as her principal enabler. Because, like alcoholics and other addicts, obsessives can't do it on their own. As they gradually lose the control they so desperately seek, they have little choice but to ensnare loved ones. My mother had begun that process back in Gloversville, by threatening on one hand that she might suffer a nervous breakdown if I wasn't a good boy and on the other crediting me with helping to pull her back from the brink each time she melted down. As a kid, though, my enabling duties had been shared with my grandparents, who lived right downstairs, as well as, to a lesser extent, her sister, my aunt Phyllis. Moving to Arizona, of course, got me promoted to Chief Emotional Guardian.

One of the sadder truths of childhood is that children, lacking the necessary experience by which to gauge, are unlikely to know if something is abnormal or unnatural unless an adult tells them. Worse, once anything of the sort has been established as normal, it will likely be perceived as such well into adulthood, and this is particularly true for the only child, who has no one to compare notes with. As a boy—and later a young man—I'd often wished my mother wouldn't enlist me in her personal, highly private struggles, but I never saw anything really wrong with her doing so. To me, this seemed a natural extension of our old Helwig Street accord, our mutually acknowledged special relationship—that I would always be able to depend on her and she on me. In one respect she and I were fortunate. Compared with others suffering from OCD, she exhibited relatively few time-consuming rituals (like hand washing). What she did require was lots of bolstering ("bucking up," she called it), especially when she suffered an actual or imagined setback. She constantly needed to be assured that everything was okay, that *she* was okay or at least would be once this or that obstacle to her emotional equilibrium had been removed. It never occurred to me, even as an adult, that such assurances could be damaging, that in offering them over and over I was making her situation worse, not better. My failure, or so I concluded, was that I didn't offer even more of them; imagining this lack of generosity, born of exasperation, was my biggest shortcoming.

What *I* couldn't see was, however, clear to others. My father-in-law had immediately recognized that something was wrong, which was why he'd warned Barbara not to let my mother move in with us that first time. Over the years, as she wove herself more deeply into the fabric of our married lives, my wife also came to understand that I was aiding and abetting her demons. In fact, she warned me of this repeatedly, for all the good it did her. She and her father came by their wisdom rightly. Barbara's mother was an alcoholic, and it was her father who, through willful ignorance and disregard of mounting evidence, had enabled her to appear normal to both outsiders and Barbara's younger siblings. Of course Barbara had no more idea than I did that my mother had OCD. Even now she's less certain of it than I am. But she'd witnessed firsthand what came of trying to reason with someone whose reason was compromised. And it was clear to her that by covering up for my mother when she came unglued, by giving her to understand that no matter what she said or did I'd never abandon her, by not insisting that she seek help, I was giving her what she wanted but not what she needed. She also understood that if my mother was trapped in repetitive behaviors, so was I. Indeed, I must have reminded her of her father, whose inability to intervene when his wife's drinking spiraled out of control had been rooted in love, yes, but also in fear, not just that something terrible could happen if he interfered, but that it would be his fault. He wasn't going to confront his wife because he couldn't, and I wasn't going to challenge my mother for the same reason. Which meant that Barbara's choice was simple and stark and diabolically unfair: she could stay or leave. What she couldn't do was alter in the slightest our doomed trajectory.

NOT LONG AFTER Kate and Tom returned to London I got a letter from John Freeman, the editor of *Granta,* asking if I had any interest in writing about Gloversville—the real place, not one of my many fictional avatars. The magazine was planning a special "going home" issue, and a couple days earlier, on the New York State Thruway, he'd passed the Gloversville exit and thought of me. If I were to take on the assignment, Freeman reminded me, the article itself would be a kind of homecoming, as *Granta* had published an excerpt from one of my early novels back in the mid-Eighties. I hadn't been in the magazine since, so the idea was appealing. I hesitated, though. Would I actually have to go to Gloversville? If so, what would I do there, exactly? Write about how things seemed there now compared with when I was a kid? See if Pedrick's still existed and who was drinking there these days? Knock on the door at 36 Helwig Street and introduce myself to whoever lived there now? Because I emphatically wanted no part of any of this. For the family memorial service we'd held that summer, Barbara and I had gotten a motel room out on the arterial highway and reserved a private room at an old-line Johnstown inn, a favorite of my mother's, for the dinner in her honor. I didn't go into Gloversville at all. Had I read the OCD book at the time, I might have recognized that my sneaking in and out like a burglar fell quite comfortably within the spectrum of unnatural and unhealthy behaviors, but that would come later. The way I saw it then, I was like Bartleby. I *could* go to Gloversville; I just "preferred not to."

Now, a year later, I was even more adamant, so when I called John I told him that yes, I'd like to write for the special issue, perhaps using some of my cousin's beam-house stories as a jumping-off point, my only stipulation being that my "going home" was strictly metaphorical. He quickly agreed, since, if I had everything I needed to write the piece, why make the physical journey? Perhaps, sensing just how strong my aversion was, he'd intuited that I had become the literal embodiment of Thomas Wolfe's famous maxim and that maybe *this* was where the real story was. With a little luck, my inability to actually go home again might bring to the theme something interesting, off-kilter, and possibly insane.

Not long after our conversation, as I worked at putting some of my cousin's experiences onto the page, my wandering eye happened to fall on *Toward Civic Integrity: Re-establishing the Micropolis,* that Gloversville book. It sat right where I'd tossed it so contemptuously months earlier, half buried now by a dozen other unwanted volumes on my personal literary slag heap. Recalling the vague boosterism of the accompanying letter and guessing the book probably had a shaky foundation of sentimentality and unguarded optimism, I doubted yet again whether there could be anything in it for me, though of course that was hardly fair. After all, I hadn't read a word of it. Was it possible that beneath my mean-spirited, semieducated assumptions there lurked a revealing prejudice? *How good could the book be?* had been my unconscious logic. *The author's from Gloversville!* And so, in a spirit of grudging fair play, I picked up the book and began to read.

To my surprise I discovered that Vincent DeSantis and I shared quite a few political and cultural convictions. It was clear to both of us, for instance, that the old manufacturing jobs that provided the economic lifeblood of towns like Gloversville were gone for good, no matter how much we might wish otherwise. We also agreed that an America that makes less *is* less. He was as profoundly interested in the new urban movement as I, and just as convinced that the time has come to start planning communities for people instead of their cars because the days of cheap energy are dwindling down to a precious few. A micropolis, as DeSantis defined it, had, like Gloversville, a population of ten to fifty thousand, and he argued persuasively that such communities might be well positioned to prosper in a less autocentric future. They had the kind of infrastructure—a downtown—that would be essential, assuming it hadn't been razed back in the Sixties. Ironically, the abandoned mills, rather than being a blight on the landscape, could become part of the solution once they'd been retrofitted to new purposes. What's more, Mr. DeSantis argued, while their next incarnation was unlikely to have much in common with the original one, that didn't mean it wouldn't be just as valid. What he and I saw eye to eye on, strangely enough, was the future, or at least a possible future.

But what a nest of thorns the past can be. "The glove industry sustained Gloversville in fine style," he enthused. "Factories were full of glove cutters and glove makers, and the sound of sewing machines and the smell of finished leather . . . were a part of everyday life in Gloversville." I, too, happen to love the smell of finished leather, but I'm able to appreciate it only because I never worked in a beam house (and my guess was that DeSantis hadn't either). But weren't there women in his family, as there were in mine, who'd sewn gloves for fifty years and, after they finally retired, earned pensions of less than fifty dollars a month? While his view of the Gloversville of our youth—it turned out he was just a year older than I—wasn't false, it rested on a foundation of carefully selected facts and memories. For him, the old days when the skin mills were in full swing were good because of the wealth and prosperity they generated. He recalled his aunts and uncles lamenting the loss of jobs overseas, then generously concluded that "in fairness to the glove companies . . . failure to take advantage . . . of cheap labor would have been tantamount to corporate suicide." Well, okay, but if a dramatic phrase like "corporate suicide" fairly describes the tanneries' untenable options in 1950, by the same token didn't their disregard for the health and welfare of the workers who created their fortunes qualify as "corporate murder"? Or, coupled with a bottom line mentality that led so many to flee the scene of the crime, "corporate rape"? Chrome tanning had never been anything but lethal, its byproducts including lime, chlorine, formaldehyde, sulfuric acid, chromium (III), glycol ether EB, toluene, xylol, magnesium sulfate, lead, copper, and zinc, to name just a few. Anyone who thinks the tanneries didn't know they were releasing carcinogens into Gloversville's air, water, and landfills probably also believes that tobacco companies had no idea their cigarettes might be hazardous to the health of smokers. In addition to chasing cheap labor overseas, the big glove shops had tried to escape—successfully, for the most part—their own day of reckoning. New environmental restrictions imposed by the Department of Labor, and later by the Occupational Safety and Health Administration, had made the industry unprofitable, whereas on the other side of the world there were no such restrictions (and wouldn't be for decades). When it became clear that Fulton County tanneries wouldn't be allowed to keep dumping into the Cayadutta Creek, they up and left rather than pay the sewer taxes levied to support a new facility specifically designed and built to safely dispose of their waste. Off they blithely went to pollute rivers in India and the Philippines, leaving behind a veritable Love Canal of carcinogens, the cleanup bill to be paid by the poisoned.

Of course in its heyday, as DeSantis rightly pointed out, Gloversville was more than glove shops and tanneries. A community, even one dominated by a single industry that hated and feared competition, still needed grocery stores, bakeries, restaurants, insurance agencies, clothing stores, and car dealerships, schools and teachers and libraries and a movie theater, but when that industry vanishes these other enterprises inevitably become endangered. It wasn't just the mills that were abandoned when the good times—if that's what they were—stopped rolling. What's also lost, as he noted, is part of your identity, your reason for being, a shared sense of purpose that's hard to quantify. People who make things are often proud of what they produce, especially if it endures. One summer my father and I worked on exit 23 on the New York State Thruway, and thereafter we were never able to get on that cloverleaf without sharing a knowing look. But sometimes people are so proud of what they make that they willingly overlook its true cost. That Gloversville once had an identity based on a common sense of purpose is a potent argument. It's been used, for instance, to explain the construction of the great cathedrals of Europe, and what were they if not symbols of communal wealth and belief? Given the technology of the day, the Pyramids are even more awe inspiring, at least until one remembers they were built with slave labor. Closer to home, the Confederacy was a case study in shared values and cultural identity, whose foundation, of course, was slavery; decades after the war that freed its victims, Margaret Mitchell did precisely what Vincent DeSantis was now doing by inviting her readers to lament the passing of those halcyon days that in her beloved South were now *Gone With the Wind*.

My mother's favorite book.

WORKING ON the *Granta* piece, I once again began dreaming about her. Not nightmares like before—no more carrying her through Kafkaesque dreamscapes, no more crazy, middle-of-the-night phone calls wanting to know when I was going to come fetch her home from Europe. In this round she and I are back in Gloversville, in my grandfather's house. I'm not visiting; I live there, and in fact have never lived anywhere except on Helwig Street. I'm a younger man, but not a kid. I'm neither married nor a parent. My life as a teacher and later as a writer never happened.

There's something oddly sweet and comforting about all this, probably because, except for my grandfather, we're all together again in a familiar and well-loved place. But it's unsettling, too, since in these dreams the house is always in terrible decay, something my grandfather would never have allowed to happen. Gaping holes in the roof allow the weather to come in, and the walls have been invaded by rot. The porches slope, and the railings have detached from their posts. Sometimes all this is something we're aware of, part of the dream's dramatic structure and plot. More often, though, I alone discover it and then have to conceal this terrible knowledge from my mother and grandmother, because we have no money for repairs. Finally I have no choice but to take my mother up into the attic to show her the holes in the roof, then down into the cellar where a black lake has formed, and she shrieks with horror. She wants to know what we're going to do. It's the only home we've got.

Though she invariably appears in them and has a dramatic role, I realize these dreams aren't really about her at all. They're about Gloversville, about a ruined house that in the slightly out-of-plumb language of dreams stands in for the town Vincent DeSantis believes can be saved and I do not. Their inspiration wasn't my mother's illness and death so much as my grandfather's. The central drama is located in the years immediately after his passing, when my mother and my grandmother lived together and didn't have enough money to keep the house in good repair. Not long afterward, once I'd brought her to southern Illinois to live near us, the house had to be sold. Later, after my grandmother's death, when I visited my aunt and uncle and cousins, I always drove by 36 Helwig Street and saw all-too-evident signs of neglect—the peeling paint, the unmowed lawn—and felt at once the betrayed and the betrayer. One year the hazardously sloping back porches, up and down, had been amputated, and nobody had even bothered to paint over the scars. The back door I was in and out of a hundred times a day as a boy now opened into thin air, a four-foot drop to a rectangle of hard brown earth that the house's new owner couldn't be bothered to seed. After that I no longer had the heart, or maybe the stomach, to bear witness, so strong was my sense of personal failure. Now, more than a decade later, I couldn't bear to return to Gloversville at all.

Maybe these new Helwig Street dreams didn't originate in my mother's death, but that didn't mean her powerfully ambivalent feelings about Fulton County weren't their ultimate source. From my childhood, her hatred of Gloversville was like the North Star, the one you navigate by, because otherwise you're lost, completely untethered. That was precisely what happened to her every single time she left. No sooner was she elsewhere—*anywhere* else—than her loathing morphed seamlessly into loss. Once she was free of it, the house on Helwig Street, the cage she was forever trying to escape, became the central object of her longing. She wasn't well, of course, but I don't think paradoxes of this sort are unknown to healthy people, and I don't blame her for being unable to resolve it. After all, I haven't been able to either.

Rather than confront my own love-hate relationship with my hometown, I simply created other Gloversvilles in my imagination. Since they don't exist outside my head, I'm free to love Mohawk and Empire Falls and Thomaston without inviting the sense of betrayal I felt when my mother and I returned from Martha's Vineyard and I made the mistake of telling her I was glad to be home, an innocent remark that for all I know set in motion our foolhardy journey to Arizona years later, as well as everything else that was to follow. My fictional towns never trailed real-world consequences. Better yet, there's no question of going back because, like the "me" of the new Helwig Street dreams, I never left. I click the heels of my ruby slippers and there I am with Sully and Miss Beryl and Sam Hall and Mather Grouse. Tessa and Big Lou Lynch are right around the corner, as are Miles Roby and his daughter, Tick. Ikey Lubin's corner store is nearby, and a few blocks farther along, on lower Main Street, there's Hattie's Lunch. They're not Mayberry, my stand-in Gloversvilles. Bad things happen there. Out behind the old Bijou, Three Mock, a black boy, gets beaten half to death for sitting next to a white girl in the theater; young, horrifically abused John Voss furnishes his wardrobe out of the Dumpster behind the Empire Grill and plots revenge; and on the outskirts of town another unfortunate boy hangs impaled atop a fence, an iron spike protruding from his open mouth like a black tongue. And the toxic stream, running blue one day, red the next, always meanders through town, touching everyone, linking everyone, poisoning everyone.

My fictional hometowns are no better or worse than the real one. They're just mine, mostly because I'm free to see them with my own eyes, whereas the real Gloversville (as I'm coming to understand, thanks to Vincent DeSantis's book) I still see with my mother's. The paralyzing anxiety I feel at the thought of returning home is her legacy. She always maintained that her one claim to fame was getting me out of there, away from the shambling, self-satisfied, uncouth, monumentally stupid people who believed they were lucky to live where they did, lucky to have low-paying jobs in the skin mills that starved them and chopped off their fingers and gave them cancer before moving shop to the Third World. When I listen to my cousin's stories about men diagnosed and maimed and poisoned and killed, part of what I feel is grim satisfaction that so little has in fact changed since he and I were boys. We share a profound sense of moral outrage that Mr. DeSantis has somehow escaped, but Greg, because he's not only lived his whole life in the real Gloversville but also raised a fine family there, has resolved the paradox that eluded my mother and still eludes me. Gloversville is his home. It breaks his heart on a daily basis, but that doesn't change the fact. His father's buried in the cemetery there, along with both his paternal and maternal grandparents, their lives and deaths tied, directly or indirectly, to the skin mills. If there were a magic wand that could make the place all better, he'd wave it until his arm fell off, and that, I suspect, is the biggest difference between us. The shameful truth is that part of me doesn't *want* Humpty Dumpty to be put back together again. I readily admit that's neither fair nor just. Though I can't justify doing so, it appears that on this topic I've taken my mother's part. Gloversville got what it deserved. So what if this opinion isn't really even mine? So what if it's contradicted by all my novels? It's still the oldest opinion I know. Surrender that one, and it would be like she was never here.

———

IT WILL PROBABLY COME as no surprise that the apartment my wife and I eventually settled on in Boston is located in the old Leather District. Just about every building there sports a plaque identifying the business that originally was plied there. We're on the seventh floor of an eight-story building, high and dry, as the saying goes, which I think would have made my grandfather smile. Leather was always a vertical industry. It went from low and wet in the beam house to high and dry in the sewing and cutting rooms, where the work was slightly better paid and less hazardous. As a small boy I remember standing on the sidewalk below and sighting along my mother's index finger up to the top floor of the glove shop where my grandfather worked and sensing her pride in him. Perhaps I understood the principle of verticality even then.

Though I'm sure he was grateful not to work in the beam house, I doubt my grandfather really thought of himself as privileged. His pay was never commensurate with his craft. The efficient new machines, together with the relentless drumbeat of piecework and the ever-shorter work season, ensured that he'd die poor. And he surely knew the work, even on the top floors, was far from safe. Sure, the tanned skins were dry by the time they got up there, but they were also full of hide dust that, breathed over a lifetime, could kill you. For years he didn't worry about his shortness of breath. He'd come home from the Pacific with malaria, and maybe that explained it. But by the time he bought the house on Helwig Street he must've

known his luck had run out. A decade later, when it was no longer possible to ignore his worsening symptoms, he was finally
diagnosed with emphysema by doctors who had little doubt
that his occupation was a contributing factor. But he was also
an occasional smoker, and he never stopped, not entirely, even
when he knew that each new cigarette reduced the time he had
left. Even if he thought he could win, I doubt he would've sued
his employers because, as he would've been the first to point
out, the glove shops had put bread on his family's table for all
those years, and without them what would he have done? How
would he have made a living otherwise? Bitterness and recrimination weren't worth the little breath he still had. In his way
my grandfather was a philosopher, and he would've wanted
me to be suspicious of any bitterness I harbored on his behalf,
just as he would've reminded me of the terrible possibility that
what nourishes us in this life might be the very thing that steals
that life away from us.

I sometimes wonder what he would have made of the fact
that the house and town my mother and I fled back in 1967
would nourish my creative life for more than three decades. I
have no idea what he'd make of my reflex anxiety at the thought
of ever returning home. The part of me that's rational knows
perfectly well that I have nothing to fear there. I'm often
reminded that many people in Gloversville have embraced my
stories and think of me as a favored son. There's no reason that
the mere thought of returning should make a frightened boy
of me, a boy who, as the Helwig Street dreams suggest, will be
overwhelmed by adult responsibilities he's helpless to meet. I

loved that house and everyone in it. I still do. Just how much was revealed one night not long after we closed on the Boston apartment. Barbara was away, and after dinner I found myself navigating through the unfamiliar television channels, stopping on one called American Life. It was playing an episode of *77 Sunset Strip,* which was followed by *Bourbon Street Beat, Hawaiian Eye,* and *Surfside 6,* all shows we watched when I was a boy. At some point I became aware of the tears streaming down my face, realizing that I wasn't in Boston anymore, not really, but rather back home, stretched out on my grandparents' living room floor, with a pillow wadded up under my chin and—I have to say—happy.

But I don't want to be a boy again, not ever.

I wonder, too, what my grandfather would've thought about my mother's life had he been able to see it all the way to the end. Would he have blamed himself as a father, as I've sometimes blamed myself as a son? I have little desire to speculate on what his specific regrets might have been, but he wouldn't have let himself off easy, which maybe is why I can't. My own regrets, as these pages attest, are full and sufficient. It's worth saying, I think, that my own feelings of guilt and remorse have little to do with my failure to comprehend what was medically wrong with my mother, if indeed I understand it now. After all, it's only recently that OCD has been recognized for what it is, much less treated effectively. What distresses me most is that I made an exception for my mother in how I normally go about things. For almost as long as I can remember, my personal mantra has been: *When you don't know what to do, try something; if that doesn't work, try something else.* Perhaps I came to this philosophy as a natural consequence of living with an obsessive. One thing obsessives have in common is they seldom try something else. By nature ritualistic, they try the same thing over and over, always hoping against hope that this time the results will be different, possibly even good. Their cycles have to be interrupted or they're doomed. Perhaps because my mother's were so clearly established when I was a boy and I'd been drawn into them so early, I never had much faith that they *could* be altered. To me they seemed like the tides: necessary, inevitable, much more powerful than I.

I now know that I should have tried something else. Not as a boy, of course, but later as a man. Because even if I couldn't comprehend what I was dealing with, I was not ill equipped to at least try something and, if that didn't work, to try something else. For the last two decades of my mother's life, I was a working novelist, and novelists, if they know anything, should know how important stories are, that narratives often provide the key to things that run deeper in us, in our basic humanity, than can be diagnosed by even the most skilled physician. Given how often I'd heard it, I should have recognized the importance and meaning of my mother's Easter story, the one where she and her sister got new dresses and my grandmother did not.

One of the heartbreaking ironies of OCD is that the myriad anxieties of those afflicted invariably have a common denominator if not a single source. A person terrified of being abandoned and ending up alone will inevitably develop a series of obsessions and rituals that virtually guarantee this precise result. What my mother, a child of the Great Depression, dreaded most was poverty, a fear rooted in her not-at-all-insane conviction that in America, poor people might make the nation's clothes, build its highways and bridges, and win its wars, but in the end they don't matter. Her need to be free and live independently was real, but that wasn't the point. What independence meant to her was that she wouldn't be poor like her parents were, like the people she grew up around had always been, like the nation itself was during her formative years. What must have terrified her after I came along and her marriage to my father failed was the possibility that no matter how hard she tried, she'd always come up a little short. That fear wafted across Helwig Street from the house where the poorest family on the block lived. To her, fear smelled like the olive oil they cooked with because—or so she imagined—they couldn't afford butter.

Poverty. *That* was the odor that turned her stomach and made her sick with yellow panic and suggested that "things . . . you know . . . won't turn out right," a thought that scared her worse than death itself. Had I understood this in time, had my moral imagination—any writer's most valuable gift, perhaps everyone's—not failed me, I could at least have . . .

Could have what? The story ends here because I don't know how to complete that sentence. My family assures me I did everything that could've been done, and I don't know why it should seem so important that I resist the very conclusion that would let me off the hook. Maybe it's because I've never been a fan of grim, scientific determinism, or perhaps it's a writer's nature (or at least mine) to gnaw and worry and bury and unearth anything that resists comprehension. But who knows? Maybe it's just hubris, a stubborn insistence that if we keep trying one thing after another, we can coerce the ineffable into finally expressing itself. How tantalizingly close it seems even now, right there on the tip of my tongue before slipping away. But no doubt I'm misjudging the distance, being my mother's son.

Acknowledgments

No memoirist likes to admit to a poor memory, but that, alas, is what I'm saddled with. For this reason I'm particularly grateful to my wife and daughters for correcting me on details I got wrong or out of sequence. I'm also deeply indebted to my aunt Phyllis Gottung, who set me straight about some events from the early years. She fiercely loved and was loyal to her big sister, and if she'd known at the time to what use I meant to put our conversations about my mother's life and struggles, she might not have been so forthcoming. At the beginning, of course, I myself didn't know where my curiosity was leading. I'm also much indebted to my cousins, Greg and Jim Gottung, for all the Gloversville skin-mill stories they shared with me over the years. Whatever I managed to get wrong despite the best efforts of my family is my fault, not theirs.

Acknowledgments

Despite my initial treatment of it, I'm also grateful to Judge Vincent DeSantis for sending me his book about Gloversville. I suspect we each love our hometown, if for very different reasons. And special thanks to John Freeman at *Granta* for nudging me at just the right moment.

To my mother I owe, well, just about everything, and to some readers these pages may seem like a strange way to repay such an enormous debt. All I can say is, this isn't a story I tried to remember; it's one I'd have given a good deal to forget. But despite my impressive amnesiac gifts, it refused to be forgotten, and I hope that that's because it's true in the ways that matter most.